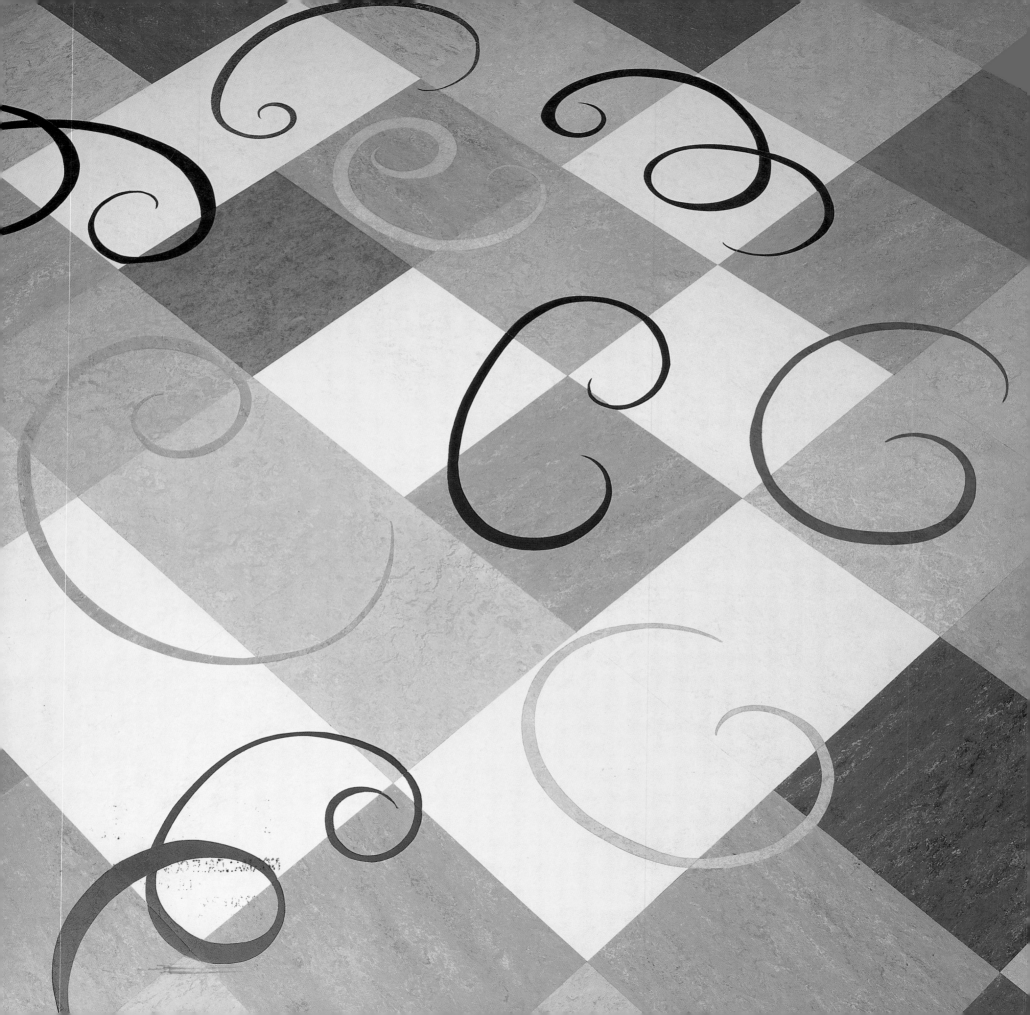

LINOLEUM

BY JANE POWELL

PHOTOGRAPHS BY
LINDA SVENDSEN

Gibbs Smith, Publisher
Salt Lake City

First Edition
07 06 05 04 03   5 4 3 2 1

Published by
Gibbs Smith, Publisher
P.O. Box 667
Layton, Utah 84041

1-800-748-5439 orders
www.gibbs-smith.com

Edited by Suzanne Gibbs Taylor
Designed and produced by Lassiter Design: Maralee Lassiter
Printed and bound in Hong Kong

Library of Congress Cataloging-in-Publication Data
Powell, Jane, 1952-
Linoleum / by Jane Powell ; photographs by Linda Svendsen.—1st ed.
        p. cm.
Includes bibliographical references.
ISBN 1-58685-303-1
1. Linoleum. 2. Flooring—History. 3. Repetitive patterns (Decorative arts) I. Title.
TS1779.L5P69 2003
645'.1-dc21
                                        2003007127

CONTENTS

ACKNOWLEDGMENTS

This book would never have happened without the many contributions of friends and strangers. I particularly salute my fellow linoleum freaks—you know who you are.

Special thanks to Suzanne Lipschutz and Martin Dinowitz at Second Hand Rose, Susan Maness at Linoleum City, Laurie Crogan of Inlay Floors, and Piera Marotto at Forbo Industries.

The following people provided catalogs and/or linoleum samples: Dianne Ayres and Timothy Hansen, Allan and Vonda Breed, Christy and Cedric Brown, Anthony Bruce, Laurie Gordon and Rick Fishman, Erik Hanson, Kenneth Heaman, Marsha Shortell, Stuart Stark, Jim Sutherland, and Valerie Winemiller.

Thanks to the homeowners, including Penny and Chris Black, Denis Cargna, Jill Collins, Rick Fishman, Troy Evans and Heather McLarty, Wendy and Leonard Goldberg, Don Hausler, Cathy Hitchcock and Steve Austin, Gayle Howell, May Quigley and Simon Goodman, and Max Wong.

This book would not be what it is without the wonderful photographs of my co-author Linda Svendsen. She also was in charge of scanning the many ads and catalogs, a labor-intensive process mystifying to those of us who don't know how to use Photoshop. I'd also like to thank Melanie Hofmann for converting those scans to a resolution that I could open without crashing the computer. Extra scanning and cat pee experiment were performed by Friederike Droegemueller and Biafra Africanus Droegemueller, the most handsome gray kitty in Oakland.

My editor, Suzanne Taylor, is absolutely the best, and I am grateful to everyone at Gibbs Smith for their support and enthusiasm.

Lastly, I want to thank my kitties, Zoe, Ubu, and Milo, for staying off the keyboard.

Jane Powell

A new period-style kitchen in a 1920s mansion sports a restored vintage stove, Malibu-style tile, and a custom inlaid floor of marbleized linoleum in a diagonal checkerboard pattern, set off by a green and yellow decorative strip set in the black border. Each corner is inlaid with an intricate design of grapes, leaves, and tendrils. (Inlay by Laurie Crogan.)

FOREWORD

This book is not about vinyl!

Linoleum is not vinyl, in spite of the word *linoleum* having become a generic term for resilient flooring. This book is about linoleum, a flooring product made of linseed oil, resins, cork flour, and pigments on burlap backing. In particular, this book is about vintage linoleum, the wonderful and amazing designs produced in this material from its invention in 1863 until its nearly complete eradication by vinyl in the 1960s. It is also about the rebirth of linoleum in the past twenty years, and the hope for a future in which this humble material receives the respect it has always deserved.

(opposite) An amazing printed linoleum pattern (#8640) from Armstrong's 1937 catalog might be enough to cause seasickness if installed in large quantities, but someone must have liked it, since this sample (above) was removed from a home in Los Angeles by one of Linoleum City's installers.

Another 1937 pattern, "Rhinelander" by Congoleum, has a deceivingly simple geometric inlay that reveals different patterns if stared at long enough.

INTRODUCTION

A couple of years ago, Linda and I had dinner with Gibbs Smith and some other people from the publishing company, none of whom we had ever met before. (Our first two books had been done with the three Fs: Fone, Fax, and FedEx. Okay, there was e-mail, too, but it doesn't fit the acronym.) Gibbs asked me what other books I wanted to write, and without a thought I said I wanted to write a book about linoleum, expecting this suggestion would be met with a certain lack of enthusiasm. Much to my surprise, his reaction was quite the opposite, which is why you are reading this.

My fascination with linoleum began at a young age, when my paternal grandparents moved from their farm to a tiny house in town. The house had linoleum in every one of its three rooms (living/dining room, bedroom, and kitchen). As children do, I spent a lot of time playing on the floor. I was fascinated by the floor—the linoleum pattern had big feathery gray leaves all over, and it was so different from the carpeting and hardwood floors we had at home. I'm sure we had linoleum in the kitchen at home, but I don't remember it clearly the way I remember my grandmother's floor.

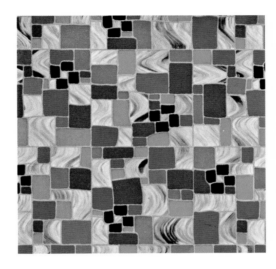

I encountered other linoleum as I grew up, mostly the marbleized or paint spatter variety, but it wasn't until I began to renovate houses that I began to come across the interesting, beautiful, and occasionally zany old patterns. Usually they were in an upstairs bedroom, an attic, or a closet, the kitchen linoleum having been replaced with vinyl.

(opposite) This inlaid pattern from the teens is made to resemble hand-painted tile. These patterns were popular from the late 19th century until about 1920.

(right) The 1930s was a bit early for LSD, so perhaps this Armstrong pattern (#21073) shows the influence of Salvador Dali. Installed, it might make one a bit woozy.

(far right) The leafy pattern of this linoleum is much like my grandmother's floor. Many of these floral patterns were produced in the 1940s and '50s, often as rugs. (Courtesy of Second Hand Rose.)

 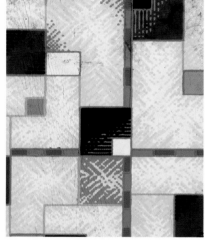 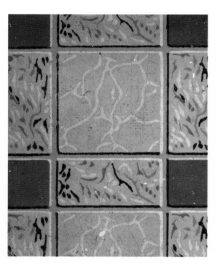 

Sometimes pieces were lining a drawer or a shelf, left over from the original installation. I began to photograph them and collect them. I found a lot of linoleum when we were working on our book *Bungalow Kitchens,* and some of it found its way into that book. Some of my friends thought I was nuts. Others shared my obsession, and they have contributed to this book.

When I mentioned to people that I was writing a book about linoleum, I would get one of two reactions, which could be summarized as an enthusiastic "Cool!" or a rather tepid, "Oh. Really?"(The undercurrent being, "Why in hell would anyone be interested in *that*?") I suspect that some of the unenthused people don't know the difference between linoleum and vinyl, especially as linoleum has become a generic term. I admit I wouldn't be too excited about a book featuring vinyl, but linoleum is somehow viewed as being lowbrow, which is a reputation not entirely warranted.

I have been puzzled for a long time as to why most people look down on linoleum, aside from it being on the floor. From the beginning, it has been viewed as a substitute, rather than a floor covering in its own right. As with many things that are considered utilitarian, it has never been given the respect it deserves. Wood, tile, stone, and carpeting are seen as luxurious, while linoleum is viewed as somehow downscale and trashy, worthy only of kitchens or dreary government offices. Certainly its practical qualities and inexpensiveness compared to other floor coverings—not to mention its once ubiquitous use in government buildings, hospitals, schools, courtrooms, and such—has rendered it less desirable in the minds of many people. God knows

(left to right) Embossing plays up the Art Deco–influenced pattern on this piece from the author's collection. The sample came from a house in Berkeley, California.

Cracks in the paint are evidence that this piece was printed rather than inlaid. The pattern probably dates to the 1920s or '30s, and was found in a downtown Berkeley, California, office building. (Collection of Anthony Bruce.)

Institutional flooring doesn't have to be boring, as shown by this printed linoleum from a Canadian hospital. (Collection of Stuart Stark.)

An even more whimsical piece of flooring from the same hospital. (Collection of Stuart Stark.)

I began to come across the interesting, beautiful, and occasionally zany old patterns.

linoleum can be quite drab and awful. However, it can also be quite beautiful. And the price differential is not what it once was: a machine-made Oriental rug, or some inexpensive ceramic floor tile, costs less now than linoleum at $30 a square yard. But you'll never see a fancy shelter magazine running a big spread on a $200,000 kitchen and raving about its fabulous linoleum floor. (If they did, it would be captioned, "Cutting-edge architect so-and-so is known for using unremarkable materials in exciting new ways.")

Linoleum is not alone as a product that is often made to resemble something else: ceramic tile is made to resemble stone, laminate flooring is made to

(above) Marbled squares combine with "overshot interliners"—essentially lines that stop in the middle of nowhere. (Collection of the author.)

(right) Though reminiscent of encaustic tiles, this 1917 Nairn linoleum pattern features ombré (shading) effects not possible in clay.

(above) A Congoleum Gold Seal rug ad from the 1920s touts that "All spilled things—even milk and grease—can be whisked away without leaving a tell-tale trace!"

(opposite) The vision for the re-do of a kitchen in a 1929 apartment building came from the Armstrong illustration on page 116. The flooring was purchased from Second Hand Rose, and the black, white, and red color scheme was designed to harmonize with the floor.

(above) Armstrong's advertising slogan, "Armstrong Linoleum for every floor in the house," advises prospective home builders to specify linoleum floors when the house is built, adding that linoleum floors like the one illustrated are "often used in fine European homes." Not many people took them up on it. Even in later bungalows like the one in this 1921 ad, there was still an emphasis on real wood. Linoleum did find its way into the occasional dining room, possibly because people actually used to eat in their dining rooms, so the ease of cleaning up spilled food was an advantage.

resemble wood, laminate countertops are made to resemble stone, wood, or even metal. If anything, it is a failing of the designers and manufacturers. All of these products are a blank canvas; they could be anything. That they are made to resemble other things is mostly because many people are looking for a less-expensive or easier-to-care-for substitute for the real material. In some ways this is misguided—laminates don't really look like wood and no one is fooled. On the other hand, how could one fail to be amused by a linoleum Oriental rug? As with many other kitschy things, some are so ridiculous or awful that they are fabulous! You might as well wholeheartedly embrace the fakeness. Of course, linoleum isn't tasteful in the eyes of the design snobs,

but who cares! By ignoring ingrained cultural ideas of taste and looking at linoleum without preconceived notions, its beauty starts to become apparent. The old patterns are from a more innocent time, before we became quite as cynical as we are today. The linoleum companies never really managed to convince many people to put linoleum in their living rooms (though they're still trying with vinyl—check out the ads sometime), but why wouldn't you want something that is beautiful, amusing, and easy to clean? Maybe you wouldn't want it in your living room, but why not in your kitchen? Are you worried your friends won't be as impressed as if you had tile, or hardwood, or stone? Are you worried that *Architectural Digest* will never photograph

your house if you have linoleum?

The upper classes have always looked down on anything popular with the great unwashed masses, and while they may be right in some instances (plaid Herculon recliners come immediately to mind), linoleum is too wonderful to dismiss just because it was once considered déclassé.

I must also point out that I am a preservationist. In fact, I am a radical preservationist. I believe that all historic buildings and the historic fabric they contain should be preserved—all of them. Not just the fancy ones, not just the city halls and the grand mansions, and the exotic parquet floors, but also the tiny bungalows and the old gas stations, the

tin signs, and the linoleum floors. Maybe it's because I'm from Oakland, California, the Rodney Dangerfield of cities, but I believe we should fight hardest for those things that "don't get no respect."

I suspect some readers will think my condemnation of vinyl is not very objective. First, I'm not a journalist—therefore don't subscribe to the notion of objectivity (not possible anyway—see Heisenberg's Uncertainty Principle). Second, I am a cancer survivor; my particular cancer, non-Hodgkins lymphoma, is tied to exposure to solvents, pesticides, and other toxins. The industry says vinyl is safe, the same way the asbestos industry said asbestos was safe, the same way the paint industry said lead was safe, the

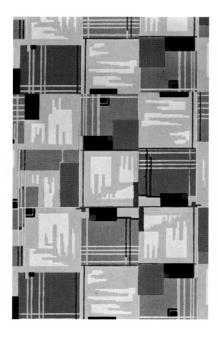

(left) Treating flooring more like fabric, this 1937 Congoleum printed design (#880) is a repeating pattern that doesn't resemble another material at all. Each square in this design measures 4 ½ by 4 ½ inches.

(center) An Oriental rug pattern called "Baku" (Congoleum #443, 1937) came in sizes from 6 by 9 feet to 9 by 15 feet.

(right) Another 1937 Armstrong geometric pattern (#5541) is an embossed inlaid design that, while vaguely tile-like, would be hard to accomplish in tile.

same way the tobacco industry said nicotine wasn't addictive. (All of those industries knew for years that their products were not safe, they just managed to cover it up for a long time, as the vinyl industry is doing now.) So, no, I'm not very objective. In any case, I also object to vinyl on a purely aesthetic basis: most of it is too shiny, too plastic, and too boring. I've used commercial vinyl tile in the past, but never again.

As usual, this book contains bad puns. I would like to point out that Linda makes up some of them, so don't heap all the blame on me. And if you don't like them, get over it.

○ ○ ○

(left) The artistry of the inlaid floor in this Spanish Revival house ought to make it worthy of a fancy shelter magazine. The citrus pattern is based on old fruit-crate labels, and a spray of orange blossoms decorates the otherwise plain breakfast room floor. (Inlay by Laurie Crogan.)

(above) Illustrations from the Armstrong booklet Dream Kitchens *for 1940 show linoleum in some other rooms.*

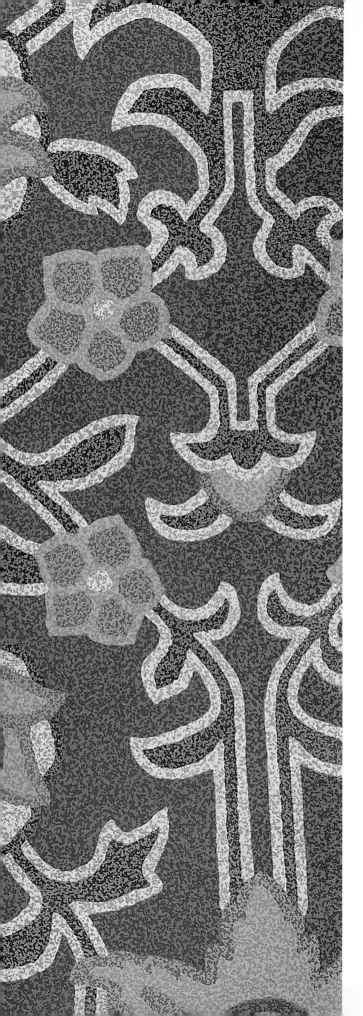

HISTORY

In the Beginning, God created the Heaven and the Earth. And the Earth was, well, dirt. Not a big deal while our ancestors were living in the trees, but once we came down to the ground we began to

notice that the ground was, in a word, dirty. As we moved into caves and other shelters, we began to look for ways to cover the dirt. At first, we used what was lying around, things like pine needles, leaves, straw, and animal skins.

The dirt also had a distressing tendency to turn to mud when wet. As civilization progressed, and we began to erect permanent buildings, we learned to bake the mud into tiles, and to use stone and wood for floors. But stone and tile, while easier to keep clean, were cold and hard, so we invented weaving, and wove rugs and mats to protect us from the cold, hard floors. And that was how things stood for thousands of years.

Things were still pretty dirty, though, and rugs and mats were hard to keep clean, as no one had yet invented the vacuum cleaner. And poor people continued to have dirt floors, as indeed many still do. This was the status quo until the

fifteenth century, when the Dutch invented cleanliness. (Actually this only applied to their homes, not to their general hygiene, and was probably a vain attempt to stave off rot and mold in a rather damp climate.) This didn't have an immediate impact on most people, but it started an inexorable trend toward cleanliness that continues to this day. The first easier-to-clean floor covering was oilcloth, invented in 1627, though not used as floor covering until more than a hundred years later. A patent filed by Nathan Smith in 1763 for oilcloth flooring describes it as follows: *"A mixture of resin, tar, Spanish Brown, beeswax, and linseed oil is attached as a coating to woven material by applying it at a high temperature."* This mixture was pressed or rolled onto cloth backing. As you can imagine from the combination of ingredients, it was easier to clean but it wasn't very attractive.

At some point in the eighteenth century, it occurred to someone that a floorcloth was not

(left) Oilcloth wasn't used only for floors. A floral oilcloth (circa 1854) covers this studded, leather-edged box. (Courtesy of Kenneth Heaman.)

(opposite) Designs based on Oriental rugs were popular in oilcloth, as they were later in linoleum.

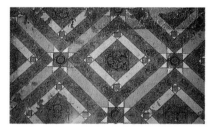

(top) The kitchen at "Briarly" in Toronto featured a simpler oilcloth pattern in the same earth tones as the more elaborate dining room pattern. (Courtesy of Kenneth Heaman.)

(center) Floor-covering fakery goes way back, as shown in a circa 1880–1890 "parquet" oilcloth with "inlaid" medallions. (Courtesy of Kenneth Heaman.)

(bottom) Much of the paint has worn off this piece of nineteenth-century oilcloth from "Whitehern," a house museum in Hamilton, Ontario, Canada. (Courtesy of Kenneth Heaman.)

unlike a really large oil painting and could be made the same way, by coating canvas with gesso (whiting, otherwise known as calcium carbonate, mixed with glue), painting on it, then coating the whole thing with varnish for more durability. The invention of the mechanical loom in 1795 allowed canvas to be made in wider widths for a seamless floor covering. Painting the canvas by hand became too expensive, especially for an all-over design, so woodblock printing came to be the preferred method.

Oilcloth became popular, even though it was expensive and the patterns tended to wear off quickly. It was prevalent in entries, stairways, and other high-traffic areas where ease of cleaning was important. It was also favored for ground-floor rooms in summer, though it had a tendency to smell and become tacky in the heat. In spite of these drawbacks, large factories sprang up to produce it. In Britain, most of these were located in London or around the town of Kirkcaldy, Scotland; around Bordeaux, France; and near Berlin, Frankfurt, and Leipzig, Germany.

CANVASSING THE NEIGHBORHOOD

Manufacturing oilcloth or floorcloth was labor-intensive. Canvas was stretched on large wooden frames, hung from the ceiling, which could be up to six stories tall

and twenty-five feet wide. First the canvas was coated with size, a material made of glue or resins that filled the pores in the fabric. After this dried, men standing on narrow scaffolding between the rows of frames troweled on several layers of thick oil paint (it had replaced gesso as the preferred coating). This was a dangerous job, and many men were killed or injured falling from the scaffolding. Later, machines were invented for this step. Each coat took several days to dry, and was rubbed with pumice stones to smooth it before applying the next coat. Both sides of the canvas had to be coated, though the front received more coats. After all the layers had dried, the cloth was transferred to the printing room, where the pattern was printed using carved wooden blocks dipped in oil paint. Each color in the pattern required a separate block, and some patterns required 60 or more blocks. Great precision was also required so that the pattern would line up. This is why hand-blocked wallpaper or fabric remains expensive to this day. Finally, several coats of varnish were applied to both sides. The process took several months because of the long drying times and the fact that water-based polyurethane had not been invented.

FRIEND OR FAUX?

Initially, floorcloths were produced in patterns based on other floor coverings such as straw matting, Oriental or Aubusson

carpets, and ceramic tiles, a trend that continues in sheet flooring into this century.

CORK IN THE ROAD

By the nineteenth century, the quest for cleanliness was in full swing, led by new scientific discoveries linking dirt, germs, and disease. It was the height of the Industrial Revolution, and inventors were racking their brains to come up with a floor covering that was sanitary, easy-to-clean, long-lasting, comfortable to stand on, and affordable. Around 1800, the British had begun experimenting with new raw materials that were being imported from their various colonies, things like cork and India rubber. The first successful result of this experimentation was flooring called Kamptulicon (from the Greek word *kampto* meaning "flexible") composed of finely ground cork mixed with India rubber. First patented by Elijah Galloway in 1844, it was introduced at the world exhibition in London in 1862, where it caused a sensation. Promoters compared it to thick, soft leather, and touted its ease of cleaning, imperviousness to water, and its warmth and sound-deadening qualities. Critics, no doubt consisting primarily of floorcloth manufacturers, pointed out that it was not terribly attractive, the color being a sort of dirty gray-brown. Attempts were made to make it more attractive by stenciling patterns on it with oil paint,

  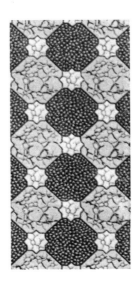   

but these suffered from the same lack of durability as the block-printed floorcloths. Within a few years, fierce competition from the oilcloth industry, along with large increases in the price of India rubber, caused Kamptulicon to fade away.

JUST THE FLAX, MA'AM

But the British inventors weren't giving up, and they continued looking for ways to make India rubber less tacky, or to find a substitute for it. One of these was Frederick Walton. In 1855, when he was twenty-one years old, he happened to notice the skin that had formed on an old can of oil paint he had laying around. He peeled it off and began playing around with it. It was rubbery and flexible, and

he realized it might be a good substitute for India rubber.

Now for a brief science lesson; pay attention, there'll be a quiz later. The skin that forms on a can of oil paint is the result of oxidation, a chemical process where oxygen molecules from the air bond chemically with molecules in the paint, forming oxides. Another well-known example of this process is rust (iron oxide). Now for some botany: Linseed oil is derived from the flax plant, *Linum usitatissimum* (literally translated "linen most useful"), which produces both fiber (linen) and oil (linseed oil), and has been cultivated since 3000 B.C. The problem with raw linseed oil is that it doesn't oxidize very

quickly. Walton wanted to speed up the process. After numerous tries, he hit on the idea of heating the oil with other substances that were promiscuous with their oxygen molecules, such as lead acetate and zinc sulfate. With enough heating, the linseed oil formed a resinous mass into which lengths of cheap cotton fabric were dipped a few times until a thick coating formed. This was then scraped off and boiled again with benzene or other solvents to form a liquid (essentially linseed oil varnish). He planned to sell the product to producers of water-repellent fabrics, such as the oilcloth manufacturers, to use instead of other kinds of varnish. He took out a patent for the process in 1860, but there were a few problems

with the method. The cotton sheets could only be used a couple of times before they fell apart, and it took months to produce enough of the resin (or linoxyn). Not to mention that his first factory burned down, since linseed oil is extremely flammable. (That's what they're always talking about when they warn about oil-soaked rags and spontaneous combustion—the oxidation produces heat.) And the oilcloth companies were not very interested in the product.

Walton kept at it, though. He figured out easier ways to get the oil onto the cotton sheets by hanging them vertically and sprinkling them from above. He wanted to find a way to make the linoxyn less

Six oilcloth patterns from the 1903 Montgomery Ward catalog suggest that oilcloth had not been completely overtaken by linoleum at that point. These tile-like patterns had probably been produced since the nineteenth century. Per square yard, #100 and #126 cost $.25, #450 and #436 cost $.28, and #974 and #980 cost $.34. For comparison, printed linoleum cost $.43 to $.68, and inlaid linoleum cost $1.38.

desperation, Walton began an extensive advertising campaign, and opened two stores in London for the exclusive sale of linoleum. It worked, and sales of the new product took off.

Once Walton took out his initial patent in 1860, it was fair game, and other inventors also began experimenting. In 1871, William Parnacott took out a patent for a different method of producing linoxyn, which involved blowing hot air into a cauldron of linseed oil for approximately eighteen hours, then pouring the hot mass into shallow metal trays, which were then cooled by blowing cold air over them. Unlike the Walton process that involves slow but constant oxidation and takes weeks, the Parnacott method took only a couple of days, though the quality of the product didn't equal that produced by Walton. Still, for financial reasons, many linoleum factories chose the Parnacott method. (And are still using it.)

Regardless of the method used to produce the linoxyn, once you have it, the steps to producing linoleum are the same. First, the linoxyn is mixed with resins (basically tree sap) and heated to produce linoleum cement. This sticky paste is extruded like some sort of industrial pasta, cut into manageable pieces, cooled, and stored for two months in iron boxes dusted with chalk, kind of like flouring the cake pan. Continuing the

cake analogy, the dry ingredients, including cork dust, wood flour (really fine sawdust), pigments, and whiting (powdered limestone or calcium carbonate) are mixed together, then combined with the linoleum cement in a series of mixers and extruders. This mass can then be granulated, made into "sausages," or sheets.

WHITING FOR GODOT
Possibly you are asking yourself, "What's the deal with the whiting?" Or maybe you aren't, but I'll explain anyway. Most of the other ingredients in linoleum are various shades of brown. Whiting lightens up the basic material to something vaguely cream colored, thus making it possible to have other colors. It also serves as filler. This is why there is no bright white linoleum—cream colored is about as light as it gets.

ROLLER DERBY
The linoleum mass, along with the burlap backing fabric, is run through heated rollers called "calenders" that fuse the linoleum cement onto the backing. After this, the lengths of linoleum are looped like so much ribbon candy (called *festooning*) in the seasoning room, a heated room where the oxidation process continues for a few months and allows the linoleum to truly become one with the backing.

The manufacturers of Kamptulicon were

tacky, so he tried mixing it with other substances such as sawdust and cork dust. Manufacturers of Kamptulicon encouraged him, since they were looking for a cheaper substitute for India rubber, which was becoming increasingly expensive. But Walton had his own ideas. In 1863 he applied for another patent, which read: "For these purposes canvas or other suitable strong fabrics are coated over on their upper surfaces with a composition of oxidized oil, cork dust, and gum or resin . . . such surfaces being afterward printed, embossed, or otherwise ornamented. The back or under surfaces of such fabrics are coated with a coating of such oxidized oils, or oxidized oils and gum or resin, and by preference without

an admixture of cork." (Apparently redundancy is not frowned on in a patent application.) He details all the machinery involved, as well as his initial ideas for the production of linoleum patterned all the way through, as opposed to surface decoration. At first he called his product Kampticon, in an attempt to ride the coattails of Kamptulicon, but shortly after changed the name to Linoleum, from the Latin for flax *(linum)* and oil *(oleum)*. He set up a factory near London in 1864, called the Linoleum Manufacturing Company Ltd., but the new product didn't catch on immediately, primarily due to fierce competition from the makers of Kamptulicon and oilcloth. The company ran at a loss for the first five years. In

Frederick Walton, the inventor of linoleum, is shown here on a nineteenth-century German tobacco card, along with a picture of two workmen installing linoleum. The card was part of a series on great inventors.

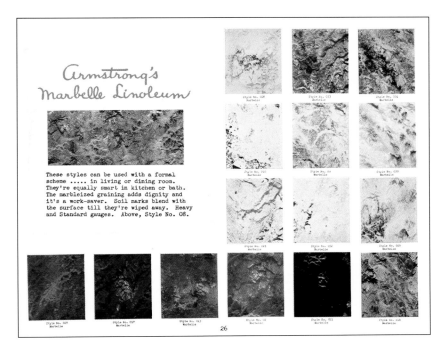

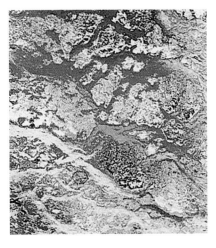

the first to notice increased competition from Walton's new product. One company bought the rights to Parnacott's patent and began producing a floor covering called Corticine (from the Latin word *cortex*, meaning "bark" or "rind," also the root of the word "cork") consisting of cork dust and linoxyn without the backing. It was considerably cheaper than linoleum and became quite popular.

Meanwhile, back in Kirkcaldy a young man named Michael Nairn, whose canvas-weaving company had been supplying canvas to English floorcloth firms since 1828, decided he wanted to open his own floorcloth manufacturing firm. In 1847, he borrowed 4,000 pounds from local bankers to open his first factory. Most people in town thought he was insane, and called the enterprise "Nairn's Folly." The bankers apparently didn't agree, because they kept lending him money for the two years it took before the factory turned a profit. He worked day and night to make the company a success, which probably led to his early death at the age of fifty-four. Nairn's widow, Catherine, and two of his sons took over the business, and it continued to expand. In the 1870s, however, noting that linoleum sales were cutting into their floorcloth business, Nairn's son (also named Michael) decided that if you can't beat 'em, you might as well join 'em, and the company began to manufacture linoleum.

That this didn't sit well with Frederick Walton is no surprise. Unfortunately, he hadn't bothered to register the name Linoleum as a trademark. He brought suit against Nairn for trademark infringement, but lost in court, since the court's opinion was that even if the trademark had been registered, it was now a moot point since the name linoleum was already so widely used that it had become generic. A mere fourteen years after its invention, linoleum may have been the first product to become a generic term, followed later by such favorites as Kleenex, Jell-O, and escalator.

Walton opened a factory on Staten Island in New York in 1872, in partnership with Joseph Wild, called the American Linoleum Manufacturing Company. It was the first linoleum company in America. It even had its own company town, Linoleumville. (The name was changed to Travis about 1930.) Walton spent two years supervising the building of the factory.

After returning to England, he began working on other products. The first of these, in 1877, was a product he originally called Linoleum Muralis, linoleum for walls. It had all the benefits of the floor covering but it was also embossed. This is the product we now know as Lincrusta-Walton or simply Lincrusta. As a decorative wallcovering, Lincrusta could mimic plaster relief or carved wood, metal, or even leather. It was a success, as evidenced by the fact that it soon spawned a cheaper imitation, called Anaglypta (from the Greek *ana,* meaning "raised up," and *glyptos,* meaning "engraving") that was made of pressed paper and cotton fibers. Thomas Palmer, who worked for Walton as a showroom manager in London, invented it. He approached Walton with the idea for the product in 1883, but Walton saw it as a threat to Lincrusta. In 1886, Palmer started his own company to produce Anaglypta. (In the early twentieth century, the two companies merged.) Lincrusta soon gained a reputation as an indestructible wall covering, which turned out to be quite true—after World War II, many of the remaining walls in bombed-out London houses were being held up by Lincrusta wallcovering with barely a scratch on it.

(above left) It's obvious on this page from a 1941 Armstrong booklet that marbled linoleum came in many colors but white was not among them. The copy notes that "marbleized graining adds dignity and it's a worksaver. Soil marks blend with the surface till they're wiped away."

(above) Conveniently, linoleum can be marbled in colors not found in nature, like this sample that probably dates to the 1940s. (Courtesy of Linoleum City.)

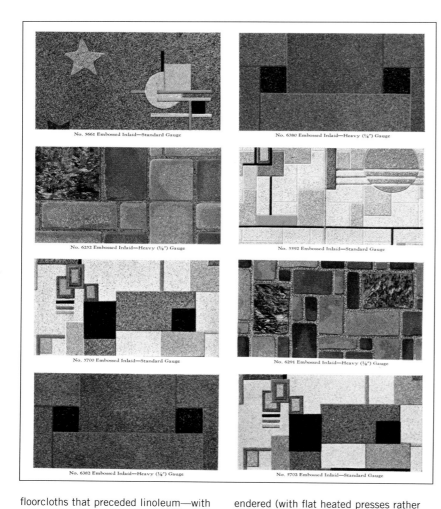

No. 5661 Embossed Inlaid—Standard Gauge

No. 6380 Embossed Inlaid—Heavy (⅛″) Gauge

No. 6252 Embossed Inlaid—Heavy (⅛″) Gauge

No. 5592 Embossed Inlaid—Standard Gauge

No. 5700 Embossed Inlaid—Standard Gauge

No. 6291 Embossed Inlaid—Heavy (⅛″) Gauge

No. 6382 Embossed Inlaid—Heavy (⅛″) Gauge

No. 5702 Embossed Inlaid—Standard Gauge

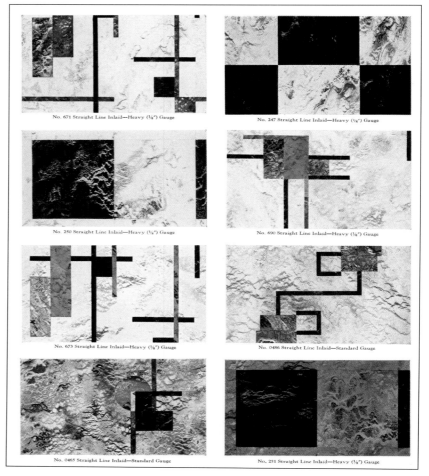

No. 671 Straight Line Inlaid—Heavy (⅛″) Gauge

No. 247 Straight Line Inlaid—Heavy (⅛″) Gauge

No. 250 Straight Line Inlaid—Heavy (⅛″) Gauge

No. 690 Straight Line Inlaid—Heavy (⅛″) Gauge

No. 673 Straight Line Inlaid—Heavy (⅛″) Gauge

No. 0486 Straight Line Inlaid—Standard Gauge

No. 0465 Straight Line Inlaid—Standard Gauge

No. 251 Straight Line Inlaid—Heavy (⅛″) Gauge

floorcloths that preceded linoleum—with the same problems. There were two kinds of inlaid linoleum. One type, sometimes called stencil inlaid or molded, involved using perforated metal trays divided into the shapes to be used for the design. Each shape was spread with linoleum cement granules of the appropriate color, and then the trays were carefully removed, leaving the granules in the shapes of the stencils. Once this was cal-

endered (with flat heated presses rather than the rollers that were normally used), the granules would fuse together and onto the backing. The edges of the design tended to be a bit fuzzy, not unlike what happens if you sift powdered sugar through a stencil to decorate the top of a cake. The second type is often called straight-line inlaid because of the sharp lines between the shapes. Initially, the process involved a lot of handwork, as

variously colored pieces of linoleum were cut and assembled into designs, rather like a patchwork quilt, heated and rolled to fuse them together on the jute backing. By 1892, Walton had figured out a way to do the whole process with a single machine.

Unfortunately, by the 1880s, Walton had lost controlling interest in his company, and he thought his partners didn't show

the proper amount of enthusiasm for his new ideas, so he sold out his interest and left in a huff. (Actually, he probably left in a carriage, but never mind.) He immediately opened the Greenwich Inlaid Linoleum Company.

At the same time, the Germans decided that perhaps this linoleum stuff wasn't just a flash in the pan, so the first German linoleum factory opened up in

(above left) A page from the 1941 Armstrong booklet Tomorrow's Ideas in Home Decoration *shows a variety of molded patterns from tile effects to geometrics.*

(above right) The crisp lines of straight-line inlay from the same 1941 booklet lend themselves equally well to classic checkerboards or interesting decorative motifs.

(opposite) A certain Arts & Crafts influence can be detected in the colors used in this 1917 Nairn linoleum.

northwestern Germany, near Delmenhorst, in 1882. This area already had a thriving cork industry, as well as a large jute production plant, so two linoleum components were already at hand. This was followed by the establishment of numerous other German linoleum companies in the next decades.

In 1886, the Nairn family decided to immigrate to the United States, where they believed there would be new opportunities for expanding the business. They began manufacturing linoleum at a plant in Kearny, New Jersey. That same year, another American manufacturer, George Blabon, installed the first American-made calender rollers in his plant in Nicetown, Pennsylvania, a suburb of Philadelphia.

SCRAPS GAME

At the start of the twentieth century, linoleum was more widely accepted in Great Britain and Europe, and the industry there was much larger than in the United States. That changed radically soon after the Armstrong Cork Company entered the linoleum business in 1908. It had been producing bottle corks and other cork products since the mid-nineteenth century in a factory near Pittsburgh, Pennsylvania. The other products they produced, such as corkboard, insulation, and cork floor tiles, were primarily an attempt to use up the prodigious amounts of scrap that resulted from cutting round corks out of square slabs. In particular, the cork dust was a problem, being not only flammable but also explosive. Armstrong had been supplying cork dust

(or cork flour) to other linoleum manufacturers, but it still had a lot of it lying around. There was also some worry that the growing Prohibition movement might cut into the cork stopper business rather significantly if it succeeded in making alcohol illegal, as it eventually did.

Armstrong built a linoleum plant in Lancaster, Pennsylvania, and began producing linoleum in 1908. At first it produced only plain, granite, printed, and stencil-inlaid linoleum. About 1910, Armstrong decided to start producing straight-line inlaid, which was becoming more popular. Rather than purchasing a cutting machine (probably Walton's) from England, Armstrong developed its own. Unfortunately, it didn't work very well, nor did the two that followed it. In 1920,

(left to right) Stencil-inlaid 1908 linoleum with a granite look once graced a hospital in Victoria, British Columbia. (Collection of Stuart Stark.)

An 1892 straight-line inlaid pattern once served as the kitchen floor of a house in Victoria, British Columbia. (Collection of Stuart Stark.)

A piece of molded linoleum from 1927 has a pattern suggestive of cross-stitch embroidery. (Courtesy of Linoleum City.)

Smaller rooms called for smaller checkerboards, like this 1933 inlaid pattern with 1 ½-inch squares in three marbleized colors. (Courtesy of Linoleum City.)

(above) Sloane Linoleum in a classic inlaid-marble pattern (#255) from 1929 was recommended for "office buildings, corridors, and much populated club rooms." Each square measured 6 ¾ by 6 ¾ inches.

(left) A 1920s Congoleum ad shows how easy it is to keep your felt-base Oriental rug clean—just have the maid mop it up! The rug shown is pattern #528 and the 6 by 9-foot size cost $9. The majority of rugs produced were felt-base, although linoleum rugs were also made. As the Blabon Company said in an ad, "Floor coverings made upon a felt paper base are not linoleum. Such felt paper products have a black interior which is easily detected upon examining the edge of the fabric."

the linoleum business having finally started to show a profit, the company invested two million dollars in designing a completely new kind of rotary cutting machine, which as one expert said, "incorporated all the good points of existing machines, left out the bad ones and added some novel ones of their own."

AD NAUSEUM

When Armstrong entered the linoleum business, there were six or seven American linoleum companies, as well as the British and European companies that also sold their products in America. There was more supply than demand. Armstrong wanted not only to increase its own market share but to

expand the total market for linoleum, which at that time was used primarily in either commercial installations, or in bathrooms and kitchens where its sanitary qualities were valued. Armstrong decided to launch an advertising campaign. At first, the advertising was primarily to the trade, but in 1917, Armstrong took the radical (for the time) step of launching a consumer advertising campaign designed to sell the idea of linoleum for every room, not just the kitchen and bath. The first ad appeared in *The Saturday Evening Post*. The company hired Frank Parsons (yup, the Parsons School of Design Parsons) to write its first decorating book. In 1918, having realized that its primary retail cus-

tomers were women, Armstrong hired Hazel Dell Brown to head the newly formed Bureau of Interior Decoration that was to provide direct personal assistance to homemakers. (This all took place during a time when the powers-that-be were trying to convince women that staying home and taking care of the house was the ultimate fulfillment in life—a battle that continues even now.) She believed that women weren't interested in linoleum per se, but were very much interested in having attractive rooms. The Bureau produced booklets and films, put on clinics, and personally answered letters from consumers.

(left to right) In an early consumer ad, Armstrong pitches their product to women, saying, "Armstrong's Linoleum offers unlimited possibilities to the woman who plans her home with an eye to economy and sanitation as well as beauty." The ad goes on to say that linoleum for every room is "one of the excellent hints on interior decoration that have come to us from Europe." In the fine print, consumers are urged to beware of imitations and look for the burlap backing. And I don't know about you, but I always plan my decorating while sitting at a dressing table.

In 1928, another Armstrong ad shows a sunroom decorated by Hazel Dell Brown, and offers a free booklet titled The Attractive Home—How to Plan Its Decoration. *The pattern shown (#5031) is called a "flagstone effect," another triumph of linoleum over those dull colors found in real stone.*

Another 1928 ad in the Ladies Home Journal *is written in first person, with Mrs. Brown describing how she transformed her house that was, she said, "without architectural charm of arrangement or detail." She goes on to describe the décor of the various rooms, starting with the linoleum, of course.*

(opposite) The 1944 booklet Ideas for Old Rooms and New *includes an idea sure to bring horror to the hearts of Arts & Crafts collectors everywhere. It describes how to transform your outdated Craftsman dining room furniture by removing the plate rail from the sideboard and cutting off the legs, stacking the china cabinet on top, and then painting it. The "colonializing" is completed with slipcovers for the chairs and linoleum on the floor.*

TAR NATION

Ah, but there was a fly in the linoleum ointment, and that was a competing product introduced in 1910: an asphalt-saturated felt with a design printed on the surface in oil paint in much the same fashion as printed linoleum, known as *felt-base*. It was cheaper than linoleum. At first, the linoleum manufacturers fought back, urging consumers to "learn how to tell genuine linoleum: look for the woven burlap back." Armstrong had experimented with felt-base in 1916, producing Fiberlin Rugs, but dropped them from the line in 1920. Nonetheless, in 1919 Armstrong was asking the Federal Trade Commission to prevent at least one company from calling its felt-base product linoleum. But in the early 1920s, the Nairn Company, which already subscribed to the "if you can't beat 'em, join 'em" philosophy, joined forces with a company that manufactured Congoleum, a 3-foot-wide simulated wood grain product used as a border for area rugs and linoleum. It was so named because the asphalt used in the product came from the Belgian Congo (now the Democratic Republic of the Congo). Alfred Erickson, one of the founders of the McCann-Erickson advertising agency (and apparently an early venture capitalist) had started the Congoleum Company. In 1903, unable to convince his new client, the American Coal Products Company, that its felt-base roof covering called Congo could challenge linoleum as a

(above) The transformation of an "outdated" room into something fashionable in 1944 results in a room that is now, you guessed it, outdated. The lesson here is this: don't make your house into something it's not, or your furniture either.

flooring product if it had some colored designs printed on it, he bought the company, added on the name Congoleum, and began producing a simulated wood-grain product. The new company was called Congoleum-Nairn, and it continued to sell linoleum under the Nairn label, while the felt-based products were sold under the Gold Seal label. Shortly after that, Armstrong gave up and bought its own felt-base company, the Waltona Company—the same company it had sued only five years earlier. The new felt product was called Quaker Rugs and Floor Coverings. It took them quite a few years to catch up to Congoleum-Nairn, which commanded the felt-base market for many years. Armstrong eventually dominated the linoleum and felt-base flooring industry, but other companies continued to compete. Besides Nairn, Joseph Wild continued to manufacture linoleum in New York until the 1930s, and Blabon Art Linoleum (Philadelphia), Potter's Linoleum (Philadelphia), and Cook's Linoleum (Trenton, New Jersey) were also competitors. There were smaller companies as well, such as Bird (in business until the 1950s) and Pabco. In 1926, the W. and J. Sloane Company, previously a retailer of floor coverings, decided to begin manufacturing linoleum under its own brand name (in the 1930s it merged with Blabon). Most of the smaller companies didn't survive the

Great Depression, or were bought by other companies.

In 1926, Armstrong began to produce embossed molded (stencil-inlaid) linoleum, having taken out a patent on its embossing process in 1925. The W. and J. Sloane Company also introduced embossed linoleum that year. Armstrong immediately sued for patent infringement. Although Sloane appealed all the way to the Supreme Court, it eventually lost. Sloane must have continued to produce the product during the appeals, as it still appeared in its 1929 catalog. After the court victories, Armstrong had the embossed market all to itself.

In 1928, the European linoleum manufacturers set up an alliance called the Continentale Linoleum Union. Represented were companies from Germany (Deutsche Linoleum Werke), The Netherlands (Krommenie), Sweden

(left) The Sloane-Blabon Company produced these leafy designs (#8157 and #8158) for felt-base yard goods in 1939. This design was also available in rugs.

(above) The Bird Company's felt-base product was called Armorlite, and they also manufactured linoleum. An ad from the 1950s shows how to re-do your bedroom for $50, using a floral print Armorlite rug. Many floral-print felt-base rugs date from the 1950s.

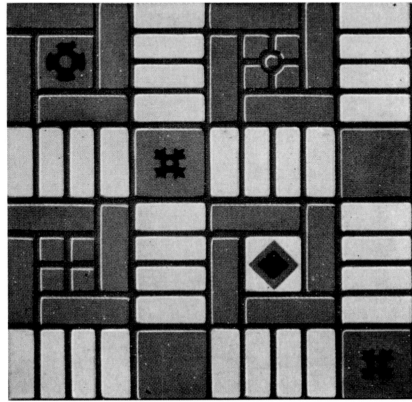

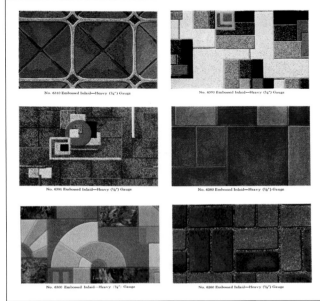

No. 6310 Embossed Inlaid—Heavy (⅛″) Gauge

No. 6350 Embossed Inlaid—Heavy (⅛″) Gauge

No. 6391 Embossed Inlaid—Heavy (⅛″) Gauge

No. 6280 Embossed Inlaid—Heavy (⅛″) Gauge

No. 6300 Embossed Inlaid—Heavy (⅛″) Gauge

No. 6260 Embossed Inlaid—Heavy (⅛″) Gauge

(above) Two embossed tile patterns (#3020 and #3025) from Sloane's 1929 catalog suggests they continued to sell embossed linoleum while fighting Armstrong in court.

(left) Embossing lent itself well to tile effects as well as to other patterns. Shown here in a 1941 Armstrong booklet, the patterns include red tile (#6310), multicolored squares (#6350), geometric motifs on blue (#6391), rust tile (#6280), semicircular motifs with squares (#6300), and a redbrick pattern (#6260).

(opposite) These rolls of linoleum wall covering indicate that tile wainscoting patterns may have been the most popular in this material. (Courtesy of Second Hand Rose.)

(Forshaga), Switzerland (Giubiasco), and France (Sarlino). For obvious reasons, Germany had to drop out during World War II, and didn't rejoin the group after the war. The Continentale Linoleum Union eventually morphed into Forbo Industries, although how that all happened is confusing, what with Nairn in Scotland becoming Forbo-Nairn, as opposed to Congoleum-Nairn in the United States (a completely separate company). It's quite difficult to keep up with the mergers and buyouts—perhaps soon there will be one giant flooring company called Amtico-Armstong-Azrock-Congoleum-Domco-Forbo-Mannington-Nafco Inc.

(above) A 1934 ad shows Crane Plumbing's Seattle showroom, which used Armstrong's linoleum and Linowall to show off their new colored fixtures.

(left) Sealex Wall-Covering (pattern #1119) and Sealex inlaid linoleum (pattern #7324) cover walls and ceiling in a kitchen depicted in a 1935 Congoleum advertisement. Depression-era desperation is evidenced in the box touting the FHA's new easy-loan plan of money for remodeling. Check out the fabulous sink and fridge!

The Great Depression affected the linoleum companies as it did everything else. Linoleum cost three times as much as felt-base, so felt-base was emphasized. The companies also did what many other businesses did during the depression—tried to stimulate sales with new designs and products. Thus, the 1930s may well have been one of the most creative decades for linoleum and felt-base patterns. Armstrong and Congoleum both introduced a lighter gauge linoleum product meant for walls, called Linowall and Sealex Wall-Covering (later known by the excellent name Congowall), respectively. Armstrong continued its embossed line, introducing new patterns. One of these patterns (#5352) became the most ubiquitous

sheet flooring pattern of all time, as evidenced by the fact that it is still being produced in vinyl. You may even have it; your mother probably had it, your grandmother probably had it. Congoleum fought back by introducing Sealex, a self-adhesive linoleum. An adhesive was applied at the factory that could be activated with water, rather like pre-pasted wallpaper. This saved on installation costs, and Congoleum claimed it did not require lining felt.

In 1928, unbeknownst to the linoleum companies, Waldo Semon, a chemist at B.F. Goodrich, invented a new kind of plastic, polyvinyl chloride (PVC), that was to lead to linoleum's eventual demise. Initially, his company wasn't interested, but he gradually won over his superiors, and received a patent for PVC in 1933. Goodrich began to market the product under the name Koroseal. It took a few decades, but vinyl eventually supplanted linoleum to become the standard resilient flooring material. Some of us think that this was not a good thing. By the 1930s, Armstrong had probably managed to educate people that there was a difference between the printed

(right) A page from Armstrong's 1941 booklet Tomorrow's Ideas in Home Decoration *features this page of embossed linoleum, with seven geometric patterns (numbers 5641, 5682, 5531, 5681, 5651, 5680, and 5530) plus the famous #5352, possibly the best-selling linoleum pattern of all time.*

(above) This sample shows pattern #5352 in the flesh.

Armstrong's Embossed Inlaid Linoleum

No. 5641 Embossed Inlaid—Standard Gauge

No. 5682 Embossed Inlaid—Standard Gauge

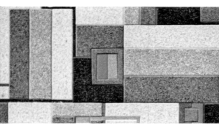

No. 5531 Embossed Inlaid—Standard Gauge

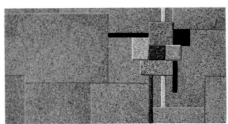

No. 5681 Embossed Inlaid—Standard Gauge

No. 5651 Embossed Inlaid—Standard Gauge

No. 5680 Embossed Inlaid—Standard Gauge

No. 5530 Embossed Inlaid—Standard Gauge

No. 5352 Embossed Inlaid—Standard Gauge

felt-base products and the burlap-backed linoleum. Because linoleum wasn't selling that well compared with the felt-base lines, in 1937 Armstrong decided to confuse everyone by offering a printed linoleum on a felt backing, called Linoflor, followed by a marbleized product called Marbelle Linoflor. Inlaid Linoflor was also offered. Still, proving that corporations don't suffer from cognitive dissonance, in 1938 Armstrong went to the Federal Trade Commission to prevent Congoleum-Nairn from using the term linoleum to describe a felt-base product.

(The Congoleum product, apparently introduced in 1936, was called Treadlite Inlaid. Congoleum claimed a patent number for it, but whether that applied to the adhesive backing or the linoleum product is unclear.) During World War II, shortages of burlap caused Armstrong to start calling everything with a linoleum mix by the name linoleum, the very thing it had sued Congoleum-Nairn about just a few years before. (Sloane-Blabon then began calling its linoleum on a felt-base product Linoflor as well—apparently Armstrong didn't bother to sue them over that.)

(above) Congoleum shows some marvelous colors in this pattern called "Cloister" (#A7443) from 1937. The large squares in this design measure 3 by 3 inches. In general, Congoleum's colors tended to be a little more flamboyant than Armstrong's.

(right) Good Housekeeping *ran this Sealex ad in 1936. It show an installer laying the linoleum directly over a tongue-and-groove wood floor, since Congoleum claimed the product didn't require lining felt. The ad also claimed that the floor would be ready to use in two or three hours, and cost 20 percent less. The pattern is called "Havana" (#A7465).*

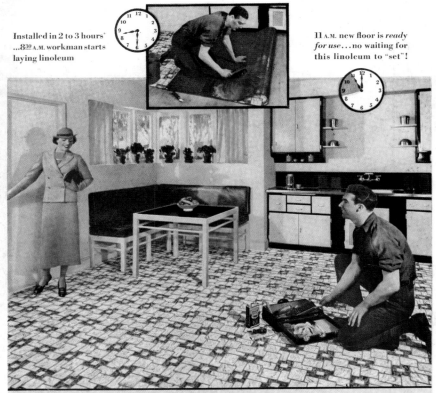

(above) Two 1937 patterns of Congoleum's printed linoleum, a tile pattern (#9653) and a geometric pattern (#9656) use the same colorway. Probably the dots inside the squares on the lower pattern would resemble marble from a distance.

(right) Armstrong showed this really up-to-date kitchen in 1942, with Linowall on the walls, plain linoleum on the countertops, and Marbelle linoleum with a green inlay on the floor. You've got to love the pink ceiling and mirrored cupboards, but those fold-down seats look really uncomfortable.

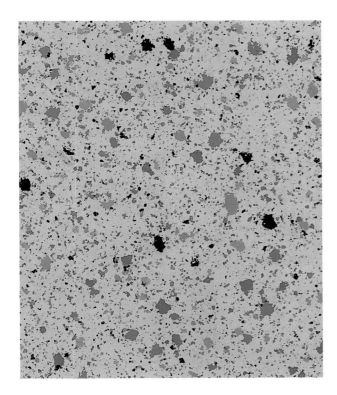  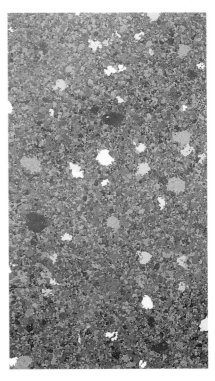

Congoleum-Nairn was busy defending its own trademark, admonishing retailers in a 1937 catalog, "There is only one 'CONGOLEUM'! It is manufactured solely by Congoleum-Nairn Inc. The word 'Congoleum' is, therefore, not a descriptive term for all felt-base floor-covering." Congoleum was trying hard not to become a generic term, and they succeeded.

(left) Almost anyone who grew up in the 1950s had this floor, unless they had #5352 instead. (Collection of Vonda and Allan Breed.)

(center) Coral was less popular than yellow as a background color for the paint spatter, although it was much more hip. (Collection of Vonda and Allan Breed.)

The German linoleum companies had gone in a slightly different direction. Influenced by the Arts & Crafts Movement and Art Nouveau at the turn of the century, they hired famous designers such as Peter Behrens, Joseph Hoffman, and Bruno Paul to design patterns. These stylized patterns gave way to strictly geometric patterns as the Germans became mesmerized by modernism. Both World Wars had a major impact on the German linoleum industry, and their production wasn't back to prewar heights until the 1950s.

Though World War II was difficult for the linoleum companies (They were forced to hire *women*!), it did effectively end the depression. Pent-up demand and a building boom had the surviving companies cranking out flooring like crazy. Many of the earlier patterns continued in production, but one of the big hits of the post-war years was a new pattern: "spatter" linoleum. Supposedly inspired by spatter-painted Colonial floors, but more likely by artist Jackson Pollock, it was the most popular floor of the 1950s. There were also some atomic-age sorts of patterns, but patterns of the 1950s were more conservative than those of the 1930s and 1940s.

(above) A granite background gave a little more depth to the spattering. (Courtesy of Linoleum City.)

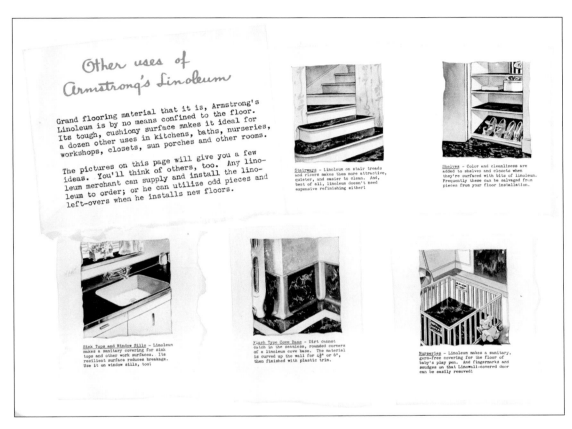

Smaller companies had started to experiment with vinyl floors, and claimed all sorts of wear and maintenance advantages. Eventually everybody jumped on the bandwagon, a lot of the early technical problems of vinyl were overcome, and, unfortunately, the demise of linoleum had begun.

Linoleum had also been used on countertops for many years, but with the invention of high-pressure laminates, that market dried up as well. The invention of no-wax coatings for vinyl in the 1970s was the final nail in the coffin, at least in the United States, where linoleum production ceased in 1974.

Linoleum continued to be produced in other countries, and could still be obtained in the United States if one knew where to look, since there was still some demand, especially from hospitals, where linoleum's antistatic and antibacterial properties were valued.

(above left) A spattered effect could also be achieved using small colored squares. (Courtesy of Linoleum City.)

(center left and lower left) Two Armstrong illustrations from the 1950s show spatter linoleum in a yellow kitchen and brick patterned flooring in a pink kitchen, complete with pink cooktop and matching wall oven. Yeah, nothing would entice a woman to stay home more than a pink kitchen!

(above right) Ideas for Old Rooms and New, an Armstrong booklet from 1944, shows a few other uses for linoleum. It really does make excellent countertops and shelf liners.

(right) New marbleized linoleum from Forbo Industries replaced the old floor of this 1920 Spanish Revival house in Los Angeles. The Forbo product, Marmoleum, comes in more than 100 colors, and in either sheets or 13 by 13-inch tiles.

(far right) A new Marmoleum installation features a custom inlay of abstract flowers. (Inlay by Laurie Crogan.)

But all was not lost. Forbo Industries, an offshoot of the Continentale Linoleum Union, began operations in Pennsylvania in 1978. In 1982, it introduced Marmoleum for the commercial market, and later for the residential market. In the late 1970s and the early 1980s, there began to be a realization that petroleum-based products (such as vinyl) had serious environmental consequences, and the "green" building movement was born. Marmoleum gained enough market shares by the 1990s to make the larger companies take notice, and recently both Azrock (a division of Domco-Tarkett) and Armstrong have gotten back on board the linoleum bandwagon.

Although new technologies such as laser cutting, water-jet cutting, and ultrasound cutting are being used to make decorative insets and borders for linoleum, currently available linoleum is limited to either solid colors or marbleized patterns.

The fabulously creative inlaid designs of the past are no longer being made, and are not likely to be, unless the companies perceive that there is a demand for them.

The rotary cutting machines used in straight-line inlaid production are expensive. (Armstrong's rotary cutter cost two million dollars in 1920—imagine what one would cost now.) Unlike a lot of other historic building materials and furnishings that can be reproduced by individual

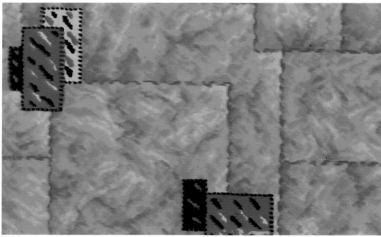

(upper left) How could anyone NOT want an amazing pattern like this 1938 piece of marbleized felt-base with geometric motifs? (Courtesy of Linoleum City.)

(lower left) Although this felt-base pattern had been covered by vinyl on the floor, a few pieces lived on as drawer liners in an Oakland, California, home. (Collection of the author.)

(right) Four rolls of fabulous felt-base from the 1930s and 1940s are only a few of the many vintage pieces available from Second Hand Rose in New York City.

PATTERN No. 1276

PATTERN No. 1358

PATTERN No. 1362

For description and prices of Patterns 1276, 1358 and 1362, see Catalogue No. P 2240.

INLAID LINOLEUMS

PATTERN No. 111

PATTERN No. 133

PATTERN No. 134

For description and prices of Patterns 111, 133 and 134, see Catalogue No. P 2244.

craftspeople or small companies, the production of linoleum requires a large factory and a great deal of capital investment. It is unlikely that any flooring company would commit to this unless there was demand for the product. The companies currently producing linoleum seem to be positioning their product as modern, trendy, and contemporary (which the Germans have been trying to do since about 1915), while try-ing to distance themselves from the linoleum of the past, which is perceived to be utilitarian, drab, and dull. Their advertising message could be summed up as, "This is not your grandmother's linoleum." (Shortly after I wrote this sentence, I learned that the vice-president of the Armstrong Flooring Division actually said that in a press release.) It hasn't occurred to them that many of us want our grand-mother's linoleum, because it was marvelous! And it won't occur to them unless we let them know. To that end, here are the names, addresses, and websites of the major resilient flooring companies. I want every person who reads this book to write and tell them that there is a market for the old linoleum patterns. Tell them if they make them, you will buy them.

o   o   o

The 1903 Montgomery Ward catalog showed both printed and inlaid linoleum. The top row of patterns sold for $.43 to $.53 per square yard, the middle row for $.68 per square yard, and the bottom row of inlaid patterns was priced at $1.38 per square yard.

Amtico International, Inc.
6480 Roswell Road
Atlanta, GA 30328
(404) 267-1900
amtico.com

Armstrong World Industries
2500 Columbia Avenue (17603)
P.O. Box 3001
Lancaster, PA 17604
(717) 397-0611
armstrong.com

Congoleum Corporation
P.O. Box 3127
Mercerville, NJ 08619-0127
(609) 584-3000
congoleum.com

Domco Tarkett Commercial
Azrock
P.O. Box 2467
Houston, TX 77252
(800) 225-6500
tarkettsommerusa.com

Forbo Industries
P.O. Box 667
Humboldt Industrial Park
Hazleton, PA 18201
(800) 842-7839
themarmoleumstore.com

Mannington Mills, Inc.
75 Mannington Mills Road
Salem, NJ 08079
(856) 935-3000
mannington.com

(upper) Printed linoleum designs like this one (#8726) from a 1937 Armstrong catalog were printed by the rotogravure process, and were cheaper to produce than inlaid designs. Most vinyl is also produced this way.

(lower) Straight-line inlaid patterns like the 1937 "Picardy" from Congoleum (#3267) could probably be reproduced today using laser or water-jet cutting technology, if only the companies could be convinced there is a market for them.

CARE AND REPAIR

Because linoleum is viewed as a utilitarian product, old linoleum (or felt-base) has often deteriorated either from overuse or neglect. Wear in high-traffic areas is caused by abrasion

from dirt and grit, indentations from high-heeled shoes, or heavy furniture. Printed linoleum and felt-base products are more prone to show wear (worn areas on felt-base will show up as black). If the pattern has worn off, but the substrate is still okay, acrylic paint can be used to replicate the pattern in the worn areas. Gouges in linoleum can be repaired with a mixture of glue and linoleum shavings (from a spare piece or taking a little from somewhere it won't show, such as underneath an appliance or behind a door), then touched up with acrylic paint, if necessary.

Water is also an enemy of linoleum. Too much moisture causes individual pieces of straight-line inlaid patterns to separate and warp, it can cause the linoleum to separate from the backing, and it can produce swelling or cause the floor to curl at the edges. This can sometimes be repaired by softening the linoleum with heat (a hairdryer, an iron on low heat, a heat gun on low, etc.). Once it's become a little more flexible,

inject some linoleum adhesive underneath the edges and flatten it with a heavy roller or weight it down until the adhesive dries.

Linoleum is also susceptible to damage from alkali-based cleaners (bleach, scouring powders, lye) that attack the cork fillers and soften the linseed oil, and can remove the paint from printed flooring. Concrete subflooring can have a similar effect if the linoleum is laid directly on the concrete. However, linoleum is quite resistant to many solvents and acids, including acetone, alcohol, paint thinner, turpentine, vinegar, citric acid, and hydrogen peroxide.

Linoleum becomes more brittle as it ages, due to the continuing oxidation of the linseed oil, making it prone to cracking. (This is even truer of the felt-base products that are basically a piece of thick tarpaper with printing on it.) Heat and patience are required to roll up a felt-base rug or piece of linoleum. It helps to have a large

Splotches and squares in bright colors decorate these rolls. (Courtesy of Second Hand Rose.)

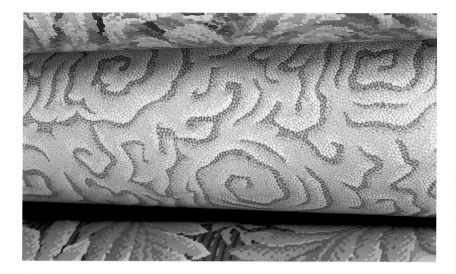

(opposite) An amazing design like this 1917 tile pattern from Nairn ought to be preserved if possible, even if only as a fragment.

cardboard tube (such as those sold for concrete forms) of the biggest diameter you can manage, to roll the linoleum onto. Roll it right side out if possible. It's best to put the whole piece outside in the sun, but lacking that, at least heat each section as you roll it, using a hairdryer or a heat gun (held far enough away so as not to remove the paint or catch anything on fire). When it's rolled up, use blue painter's tape to hold it closed.

Often old linoleum is dirty or covered with layers of built-up wax. Use only pH neutral cleaners, and test them first on a small area. If stripping wax is necessary, either a solvent-based stripper or one of the newer citrus-based strippers can be used, but test first. Printed linoleum and felt-base products were usually coated with varnish or shellac. Shellac comes off easily with denatured alcohol. Varnish is a little more difficult—most products that will remove the varnish will also remove the paint.

Turpentine will remove the varnish but only soften the paint. Turpentine is toxic, so wear a respirator and ventilate the room. Once the linoleum has been cleaned and repaired, it should be given a protective coating, such as acrylic sealer, wax, or shellac. According to Twentieth Century Building Materials, polyurethane shouldn't be used.

The continuing oxidation of the linseed oil can cause the linoleum to darken in areas not exposed to light such as under appliances or furniture. The darkening can be reversed by exposure to daylight or fluorescent light for a few days.

(above right) Two people in evening dress are meant to suggest luxuriousness for the "Gentian" (#396) felt-base rug in a 1926 Congoleum ad. Felt-base becomes very brittle with age and tears easily, so it's important for it be warm before being rolled up.

(above left) If rolled up while warm, linoleum or felt-base can live to see another day, like these three rolls at Second Hand Rose in New York City.

The dirt on this piece of felt-base should come off easily with gentle scrubbing.

Since most historic linoleum patterns cannot be replaced, it is important to conserve as much of the old linoleum as possible. If it is too far gone, and has to be replaced, at least document what is there, and save some of it (it makes great drawer liners and shelf paper).

New linoleum will last a long time if properly cared for. Surface dust can be removed with a dust mop or by sweeping or vacuuming. The floor can be damp-mopped periodically using only pH-neutral cleaners, and an acrylic sealer applied maybe once a year. If you're into more work, or have household help, you can use wax. Trust me, the right marbleized pattern hides so much dirt that damp-mopping every six months will be plenty, and no one will be able to tell. Also, because of its anti-static properties, linoleum doesn't attract dirt. Most new linoleum comes already sealed with a thin coat of lacquer or something similar, but a coat of wax or sealer is still recommended.

Felt-base flooring in a pattern combining random tile and flagstone with floral insets is still in use in an unrestored kitchen. Felt-base does not wear as well as linoleum because the patterns are printed on the surface.

(opposite) The paint spilled on this piece of printed felt-base might come off with Goof-Off or a similar product, if the paint happens to be latex. Oil-base paint might be softened enough with turpentine that it could be gently scraped off, or scrubbed off with fine steel wool. (Courtesy of Marsha Shortell.)

Just for amusement, because the names are so great, here are a few of the cleaning products recommended by Congoleum in 1932:

Briten-All
Cleanol
Clean-O-Shine
Clean-Zit
Cleeno Cleaner
Dir-Toff Liquid Cleanser
Flaxoap
Florklenz
Flu-Id-Zip
Germo-Sparkolene
Gleamite
Gloss-O-Sass
Kleanglow
Kleansall
Kleanshyne
Kleenital
Lin-O-Aid
Lino-San
Lino-Shine
Linowype
Maid O' the Mist
Murphy's Oil Soap *(still available)*
Neutraloid
Sass-O-Glo
Scrubzol
Shine Zit
Soapeze
Surfa-Saver
Washine
Zoleo

o   o   o

PATTERNS

Because many linoleum patterns were produced for decades, this section is divided by types of patterns rather than when they were made, though dates have been included if they are known.

Mock Around the Clock

As linoleum has mostly been viewed as a substitute for some other kind of flooring, rather than a flooring in its own right, it is no wonder that for the most part the patterns tend to mimic other flooring materials. Architecture critic Ada Louise Huxtable called this sort of thing "substitute gimcrackery" and she didn't mean that in a good way.

Tile

The most popular pattern is imitation ceramic tile. All kinds of tile are represented, from basic 4 by 4 or 6 by 6 squares, to encaustic tile, mosaic tile, hexagons, octagons, rectangles, and every possible combination thereof. Straight-line inlaid, stencil-inlaid, printed linoleum, and printed felt-base all featured tile.

(above) Rectangular tiles form a pinwheel around a center square in this mosaic sample. (Courtesy of Linoleum City.)

(opposite) In 1889, this complex mosaic pattern was laid on the floors of the Supreme Courthouse in Victoria, British Columbia. (Collection of Stuart Stark.)

Dinner: the South American way . . .

A dining room that effectively captures all the elegance and lavish décor for which our "good neighbors" are famous, yet it can be duplicated right in your own home. Here are decorative ideas aplenty—the antique Italian table painted white, and chairs upholstered in turquoise rough weave satin, the white plaster scrolls on the walls and over the draperies, the handsome candelabra, the wall niche with its lush bouquet—all these things lend an authentic Latin-American air to the room. And the floor of Armstrong's Embossed Linoleum No. 6310 is itself in character. This tile-like design in brick and rust-colored tones might actually have been selected by a South-American decorator to grace the floors of a fine hacienda. The border effect is composed of Plain Terra Cotta Linoleum No. 25 accented with a Silver Gray (No. 26) Linostrip.

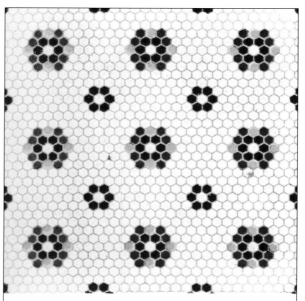

No. 7090—Felt-Base Yard Goods
A Quality
2 yards wide only

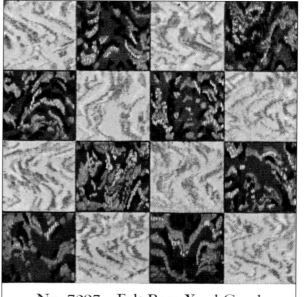

No. 7097—Felt-Base Yard Goods
A Quality
2 yards and 3 yards wide

(above) Sometimes one just has to admire the copywriters who came up with this description for a 1941 Armstrong booklet: " . . . might actually have been selected by a South American decorator to grace the floors of a fine hacienda." Well, yes, pattern #6310 does have a vague Spanish air. But the rest of the décor is so perfectly dreadful that it's absolutely fabulous.

(right) Sloane offered a lovely imitation of the ubiquitous 1-inch white hexagon tiles with pattern #7090 in its 1929 catalog. Also shown is a green and white "marble" checkerboard (#7097).

Encaustic tile patterns like this 1917 version by Nairn were popular in the nineteenth century and the first two decades of the twentieth.

(opposite) A seriously marbled checkerboard with insets of green, called "Tarentine" (#6066), was also shown in red, black, gray, and blue in the 1937 Congoleum catalog.

Stone

Ever since Frederick Walton figured out how to make granite and marbled linoleum by combining different colored linoleum granules, these and other kinds of ersatz stone have been a fundamental part of all linoleum product lines. Marbled was and is the most popular—in fact, marbled is just about the only pattern available today in linoleum, but granite, flagstone, cobblestones, and pebbles also appeared.

(left) It's amazing how many patterns are possible using only squares and rectangles, like this autumn-toned sample. (Courtesy of Linoleum City.)

(above) Nairn advertised several tile-like inlaids in the 1925 Saturday Evening Post. Part of the copy reads, "An improved process of manufacture has placed this beautiful flooring in reach of every purse."

(opposite) Flagstone was a popular stone motif; it was thought to give more of an outdoor look to sunporches and halls, or a more rustic look to kitchens. This sample is a 1933 pattern in reds and browns.

No. 1230—"Clearline" Inlaid—C Gauge
2 yards wide only

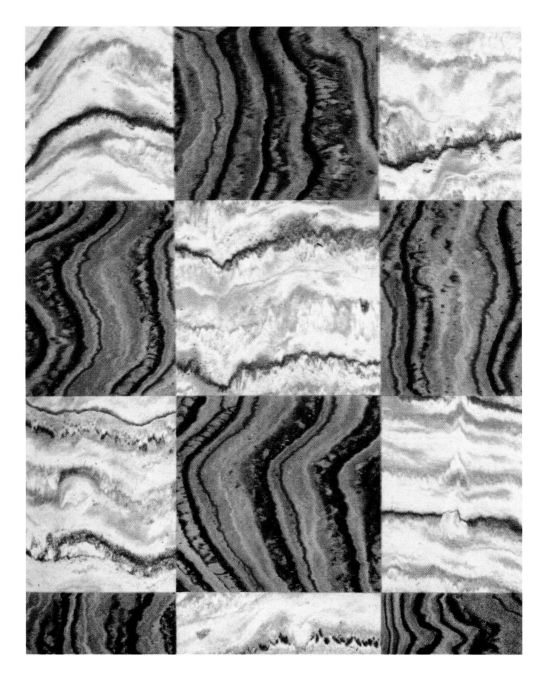

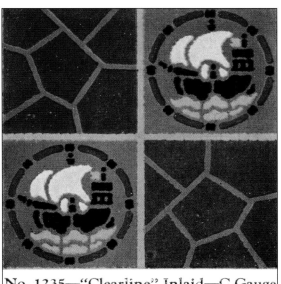

No. 1235—"Clearline" Inlaid—C Gauge
2 yards wide only

(above) The 1929 Sloane catalog featured a checkerboard of mosaic squares interspersed with plain squares (#1230), as well as a flagstone pattern alternating with inlaid ships (#1235).

(left) In their 1937 catalog, Armstrong was showing this onyx-like checkerboard (#152), part of the "Handmade Marble Inlaid" line.

(opposite) Another Nairn parquet pattern from 1917 is almost cartoon-like in its depiction of the wood grain. Austrian-born designer Ettore Sottsass would have loved it.

Wood

Patterns resembling wood were often sold as borders for linoleum rugs, although patterns mimicking parquet were advertised for all-over use in formal rooms (that was mostly wishful thinking on the manufacturers' part). Wood patterns always look fake. Don't let it bother you—embrace the fakeness.

Linoleum in parquet patterns was promoted for formal rooms, like this 1917 Nairn example. It may have looked slightly less fake on the floor than it does close up, but not much.

Come out of that fantasy world where everything from the 1950s is well-designed and oh-so-retro, and decide whether the diamond jaspé floor makes this room worse or better.

(opposite) Flowers have been a design motif for centuries, so it's hardly surprising they appeared in linoleum and felt-base as well. This pattern probably dates to the 1940s or 1950s. (Courtesy of Linoleum City.)

Brick

Brick doesn't make for an easy-care floor in real life, so maybe that's why it was popular in linoleum. (There are worse things than brick: the kitchen floor in architect Frank Gehry's home is asphalt paving. I always wondered what his wife thought about that.)

Jaspé

The name of this striated pattern refers to its resemblance to the mineral jasper, sometimes known as chalcedony.

Straw

Both oilcloth and linoleum were sometimes printed to resemble straw (or other fiber) matting. As with brick, the linoleum version was a lot easier to keep clean.

(above) An unusually colored brick pattern in embossed molded linoleum was used in a Portland, Oregon, billiard parlor, and the owners liked it so much they brought the leftovers home and pieced it together as flooring for their kitchen. The home's current owner uncovered and restored the floor, which was buried under several layers of vinyl.

(above) Jaspé and marble combine in myriad ways on this piece. (Courtesy of Second Hand Rose.)

(opposite) Japanese influence is evident in a 1934 floral with cherry blossoms. (Courtesy of Linoleum City.)

Florals

Flowers were particularly prevalent as a design element on nineteenth-century linoleum in all-over patterns. In the twentieth century, florals tended to be limited to rugs rather than sheet goods, although there were exceptions. Floral borders were often found on what were called passage coverings, narrow runners made for hallways.

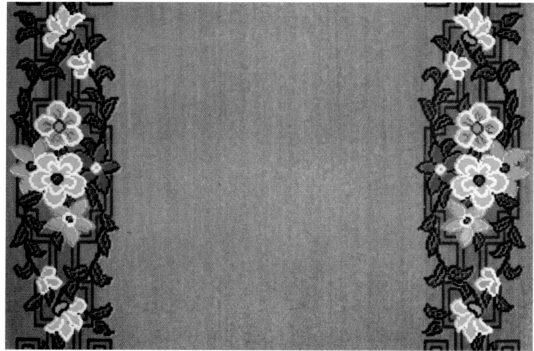

Two passage linoleums from Armstrong's 1937 catalog show a Greek key border (#100) and a floral border (#S132).

Flowers also appeared in tile-like patterns, such as these shown in the 1908 decorating catalog of the Frank Betz Company.

(opposite) Sometimes floral patterns didn't involve flowers at all, only leaves, like this piece with oak leaves in the background and some other sort of leaves in the foreground. (Courtesy of Linoleum City.)

(left) Floral borders were often used on passage linoleum, although other designs were used as well, as shown in these two rolls at Second Hand Rose in New York City.

(above) This 1937 Armstrong design is a folk art–influenced hooked rug pattern (#5490).

Carpets/Rugs

What could be finer than a linoleum Oriental carpet? No worries about the cat throwing up on it, or a guest spilling red wine on it, and with all the loveliness of Oriental design? The majority of the rugs were felt-base, not linoleum. Besides the popular Oriental designs, there were Chinese designs, folk designs, designs especially for children's rooms or nurseries, as well as most of the designs found in sheet goods, only with a border.

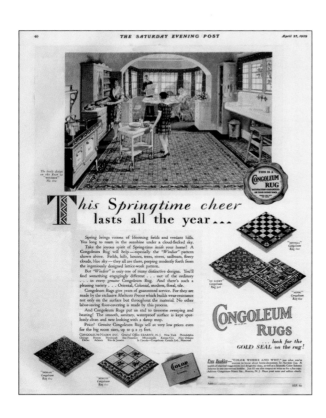

Congoleum advertised their felt-base rugs in the 1929
Saturday Evening Post. *The "Windsor" pattern (#602) shown in the kitchen features (according to the copy), "Fields, hills, houses, trees, rivers, sailboats, fleecy clouds, blue sky . . . peeping modestly forth from the ingeniously designed lattice-work pattern." By this time Congoleum had their own decorator, one Harriette Lea, and offered her booklet,* Color Where and Why.

Armstrong's 1937 felt-base rug (#4875), showing a Chinese pattern of flowers and butterflies on a leafy tan background.

Pattern #4293 is a classic Oriental carpet design offered by Armstrong in 1937. It came in sizes from 4 by 6 feet, all the way up to 11 by 15 feet.

Pattern #0180 is a medallion-style Oriental rug from the "Crescent" line of 1937.

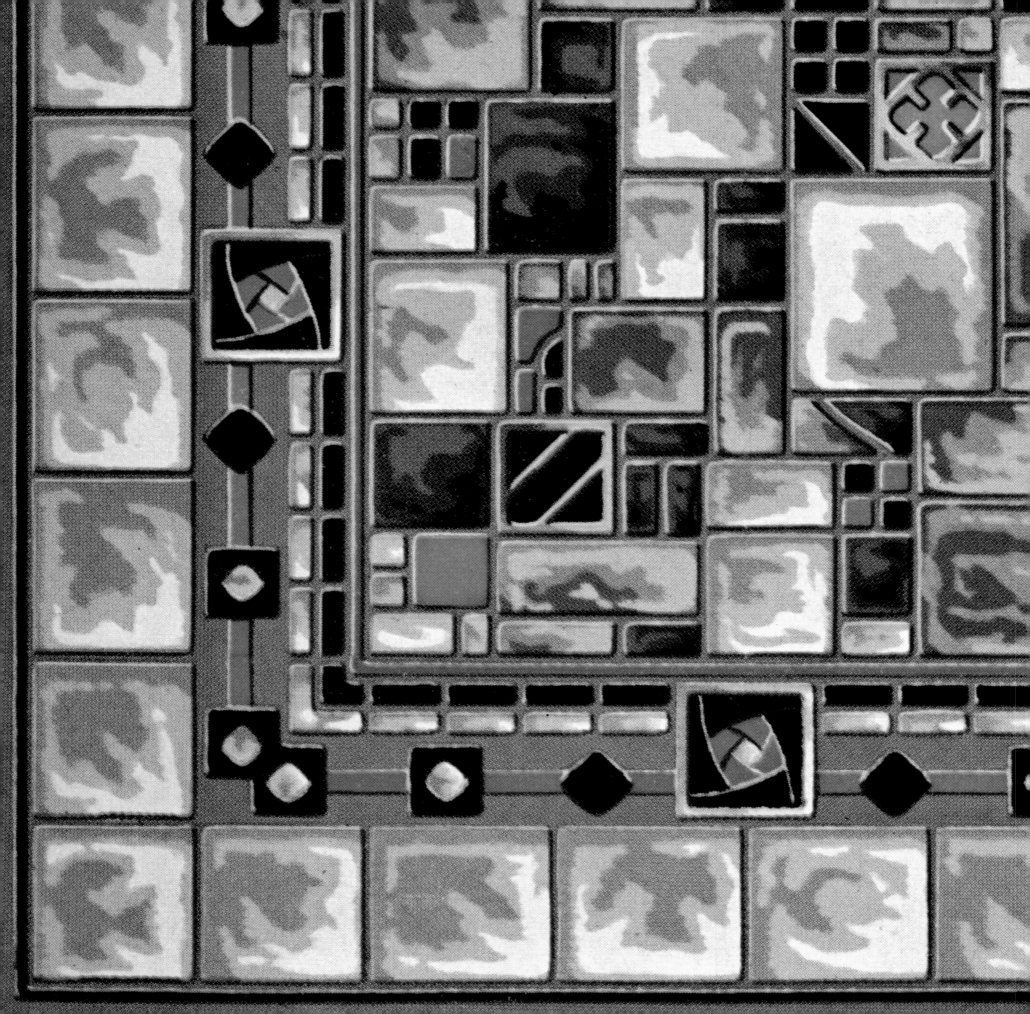

(opposite) The influence of Charles Rennie Mackintosh can still be seen in the stylized roses that border another Armstrong rug from 1937 (#4625). The squares in the border are suggestive of glass blocks.

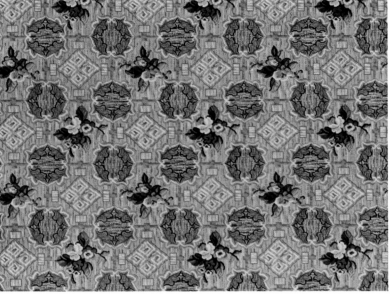

(left) Rug pattern #4567 has a Japanese look with its sprays of flowers on a mottled tan background.

(above right) A more muted look is shown in the 1937 "Hawthorne" by Congoleum (#452). This rug came in sizes up to 9 by 15 feet.

(below right) If you can have a fake Oriental rug there's no reason you can't have a fake braided rug as well. Perfect for that Early American interior. (Collection of the author.)

(left) Is it a hooked rug or a chenille bedspread? Whatever it is, this piece of felt-base was recently removed from a house in Oakland, California. (Collection of the author.)

(above) I'm not sure they were still making felt-base rugs in the 1970s, but this green "shag" carpet would certainly be just the thing for that '70s revival that's probably on the horizon. (Collection of the author.)

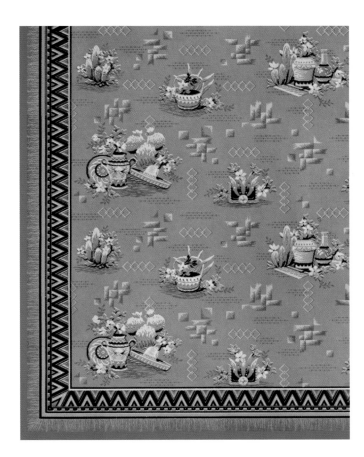

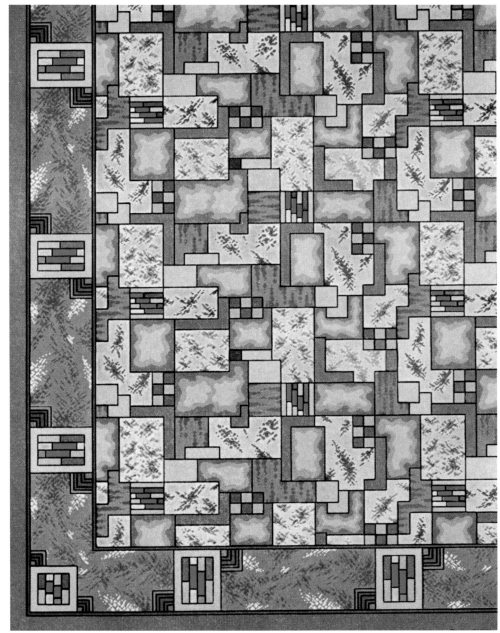

(above) Sloane-Blabon offered a "Service-Bond" rug with a Mexican flavor in two colorways, green and tan, in their 1939 catalog. "Service-Bond" was their higher-priced felt-base line, while the "Calmar" line was more moderately priced.

(right) Here's a fun 1937 tile pattern (#0160) in the lower-priced "Crescent" line by Congoleum.

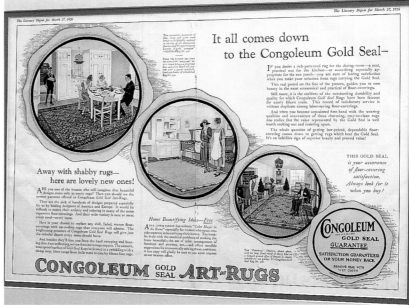

(opposite) Another version of little Jack Horner, this time with Goldilocks and the Three Bears. The middle rug has cute animals in pink and blue, and the right hand rug features poodles, ducks, and other animals, with a border of straw matting. (Courtesy of Second Hand Rose.)

(above) Three different blue rugs were featured in this 1926 Congoleum advertisement. At that point they were still calling them "art rugs." (Courtesy of Linoleum City.)

(left) Little Jack Horner combines with other nursery rhyme characters in the border, as well as various game boards in the field, in a 1937 Armstrong felt-base rug (#4595) for children's rooms.

(left) A hand-drawn map of North America decorates this remarkable felt-base rug, complete with images indicative of the various states in the U.S., along with a border of stagecoaches and wagon trains. (Courtesy of Second Hand Rose.)

(opposite) The bottom portion of the same rug, complete with jumping fish in the Gulf of Mexico. This rug is quite valuable. (Courtesy of Second Hand Rose.)

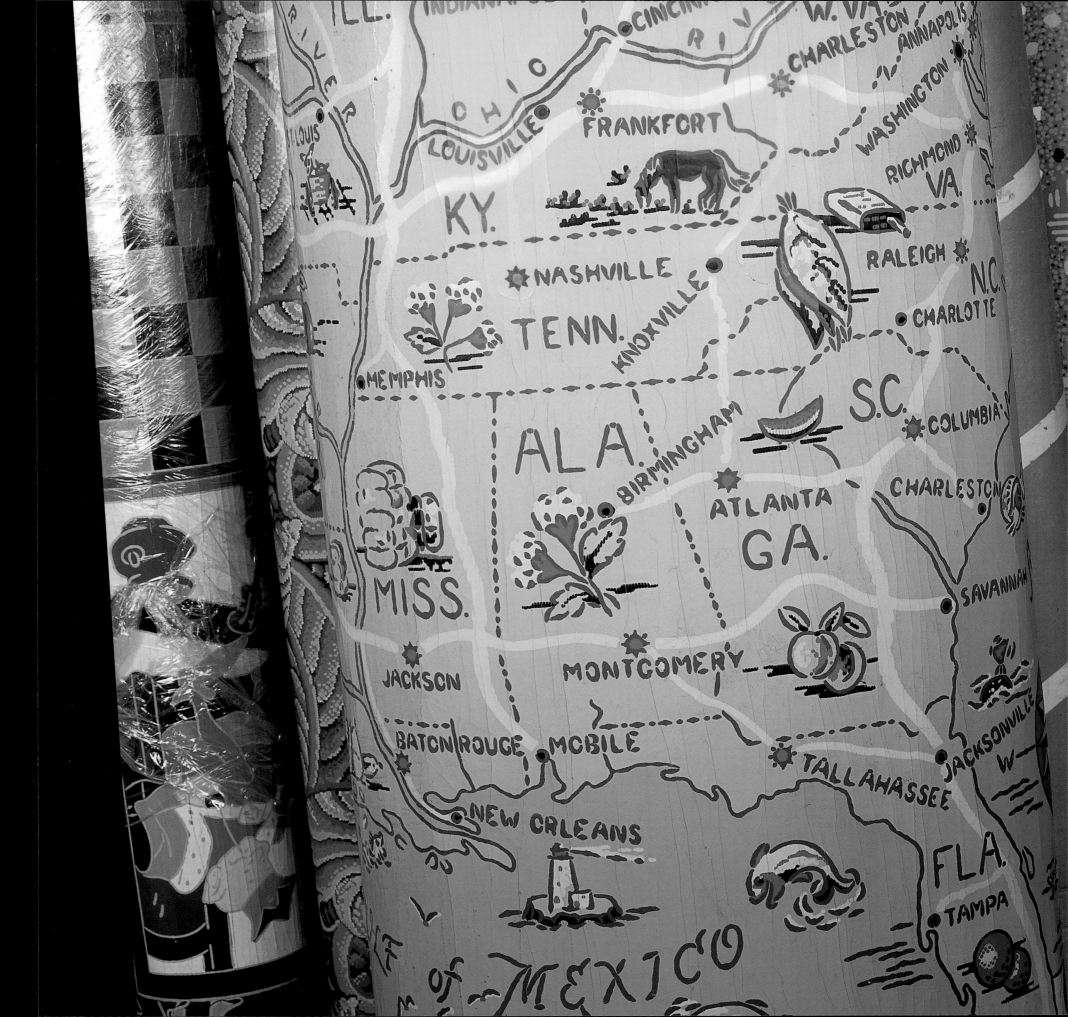

Checkerboards

Checkerboards of alternating dark and light colors have been a design motif for centuries, and lent themselves well to both solid colors, and blocks of the various other faux patterns. This is one of the few old patterns that can be easily duplicated today by using different colored linoleum tiles.

(above left) Congoleum-Nairn used this illustration of the Scotch Plains, New Jersey, home of architect John M. Hatton to promote their inlaid floors in 1926. A checkerboard pattern called "Belflor" (#2047/8) in mottled gray-and-black squares is used in a dining room and an entry hall.

(above center) In the 1950s, Armstrong bought a farmhouse outside Lancaster, Pennsylvania, and proceeded to ruin its 1920s kitchen (lower left), although they did admit that the old linoleum was still serviceable. The new floor in cream, red, and gray is kind of fun, but the window treatment is terrifying.

(above right) Congoleum advertised their pointillist-influenced "Jeweltones" felt-base in 1950, proclaiming, "Costs you less than $10 for an average-size room." They were not specific as to what was meant by "average-size."

(opposite) Two shades of green marble in 5-inch squares are separated by gray "grout" in a piece of 1922 linoleum. (Courtesy of Linoleum City.)

Ulterior Motifs

Then there are the patterns that are hard to clas-
sify because they don't particularly resemble
anything else, they were uncommon, or they're
just plain weird. There were a few designs in
every decade that weren't an imitation of something else, and particularly the 1920s to the
1940s was a time when the designers looked at
linoleum as a large blank canvas onto which they
could put almost anything with a repeating pattern. Patterns known as jigsaw, random tile,
overshot interliners, etc. were prevalent in the
1930s and 1940s, while the 1950s brought
many space-age patterns to the fore.

*(above) Hazel Dell Brown strikes again in 1944
with this "Pennsylvania Dutch" kitchen, which
apparently does not have a refrigerator since that
space is taken up by a desk and a
magazine rack. But the floor is a very cool
embossed inlaid pattern (#5530).*

*(right) Another pointillist pattern (this one from
1908) once graced the floors of St. Joseph's
Hospital in Victoria, British Columbia.*

*(opposite) Pattern #5530 in real life is remarkably
contemporary. (Courtesy of Linoleum City.)*

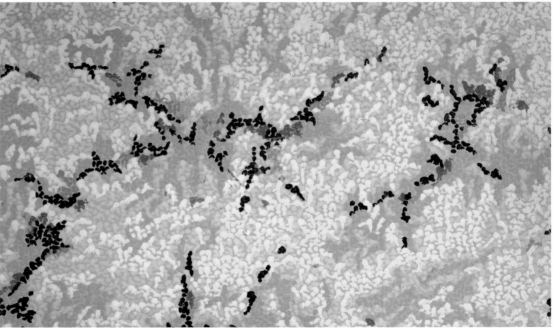

Rather more tasteful, this 1944 kitchen by Hazel Dell Brown has a straight line inlaid (#0376) with "overshot interliners" on the floor, peach Linowall (#705) on the walls, and black linoleum on the countertops. The sheer pink curtains are a bit questionable though.

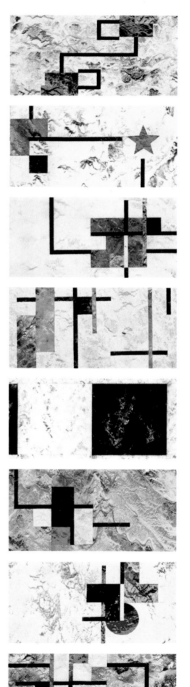

(above left) Brightly colored, vaguely Southwestern designs are overlaid on a marbleized checkerboard in this Armstrong felt-base design (#2851) from 1937.

(above center) More "overshot interliners" add interest to this 1937 random tile pattern (#5522) from Armstrong.

(stacked) Lots of "overshot interliners" in the designs of this Armstrong straight-line inlay from 1941 include pattern numbers 0488, 252, 0456, 0437, 0375, 0466, 670, and 0376.

(above) A variety of patterns, including (left to right) a 1950s floral, an Oriental floral, a pattern reminiscent of the Rocky and Bullwinkle credits, and a matchstick pattern (possibly from the '50s.) (Courtesy of Second Hand Rose.)

(left) Wave forms and a chambered nautilus might make this pattern perfect for a bathroom. (Courtesy of Second Hand Rose.)

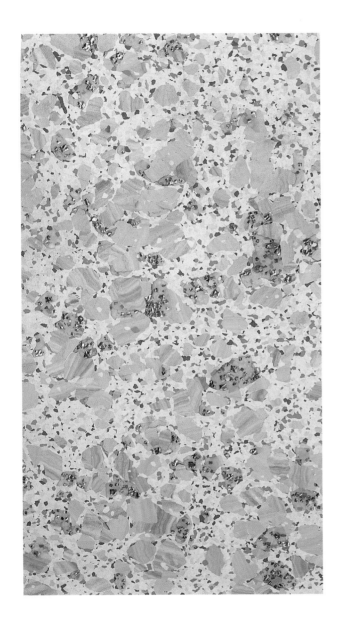

(above) Gold, silver, and copper metallic accents dot this piece that probably dates to the 1960s. (Courtesy of Linoleum City.)

(right) Splotches and squares in bright colors decorate these rolls. (Courtesy of Second Hand Rose.)

(above) Another 1941 kitchen from Hazel Dell Brown bases its décor on the "Chinese maze pattern overlaid with colored blocks" in the floor (#0488). The sink counter and the table are covered with marbleized linoleum (#017), and the walls are covered with Linowall (#770).

(left) Aztec motifs are used for this 1937 Armstrong pattern (#6300) in embossed inlaid linoleum.

New Linoleum

Linoleum is still being made, and although there are only solid colors or variations on marble instead of the old fabulous patterns, there are a few ways around that. For one thing, the companies produce borders and insets that you can use to jazz up your installation. (Some of them will do custom borders and insets.) A simple geometric design would be possible (though labor-intensive) for a do-it-yourself job with linoleum tiles. And there's nothing to stop you from ordering some plain linoleum and stenciling, silk-screening, or woodblock printing a design on it. You could even put a linoleum-block print on your linoleum! If you're not interested in doing it yourself, a talented installer can do a custom inlay that will make your floor unlike any other.

(above) Many installers can do custom inlays, like this bamboo pattern set into a black marbleized floor. (Inlay by Laurie Crogan.)

(right) Some of the effects possible using precut inlays (Linosets) and precut linoleum strips (Linostrips) were shown in a 1944 Armstrong booklet.

Special floor effects in Armstrong's Ready-Cut Linosets

BELOW YOU SEE a number of especially pleasing floor designs achieved with Linosets. Combined with Linostrips—ready-cut strips of linoleum—they provide the beauty of custom-designs at a most modest cost. Get paper and pencil and start designing new individualized floors for your home today! It's grand fun!

The graceful, flowing lines of the Flamingo Linoset form a decorative and pleasing design. The Linoset could be effectively used in the center of the floor in a small bath or placed in each corner of a sun porch.

Breakfast rooms and kitchens may be enlivened by the warm colors and charming design of the Dinner Service Linoset. Many of the other distinctive floor treatments shown on this page may also be used with this Linoset.

Strong red and blue predominate in this gay Mixing Bowl Linoset. Placed in the floor on diagonal lines, it may cut across the center of a small room or be used to decorate the corners of a large kitchen.

Nautical colors were chosen for the Ship Linoset. The color combination shown here will cheer many a room, or add an out-of-doors flavor to a den or game room. The Linoset shown here is equally good in Linowall.

A dressing room, a downstairs lavatory or powder room—all will be more interesting and colorful if this cunning Sea Horses Linoset is added to the floor. The dainty colors also make this Linoset good for baths.

The cool colors of the Porpoise Linoset are restful and the design is adapted to use in many different rooms, such as baths, powder rooms, playrooms, and so forth. This floor design is particularly attractive.

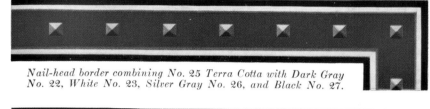

Nail-head border combining No. 25 Terra Cotta with Dark Gray No. 22, White No. 23, Silver Gray No. 26, and Black No. 27.

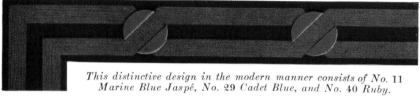

This distinctive design in the modern manner consists of No. 11 Marine Blue Jaspé, No. 29 Cadet Blue, and No. 40 Ruby.

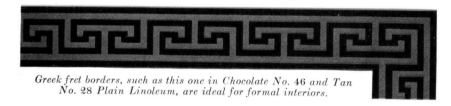

Greek fret borders, such as this one in Chocolate No. 46 and Tan No. 28 Plain Linoleum, are ideal for formal interiors.

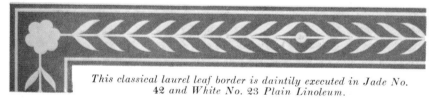

This classical laurel leaf border is daintily executed in Jade No. 42 and White No. 23 Plain Linoleum.

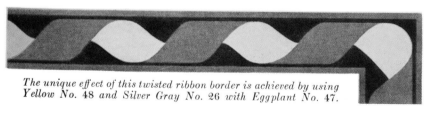

The unique effect of this twisted ribbon border is achieved by using Yellow No. 48 and Silver Gray No. 26 with Eggplant No. 47.

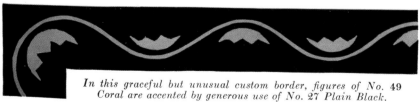

In this graceful but unusual custom border, figures of No. 49 Coral are accented by generous use of No. 27 Plain Black.

SEALEX LINSIGNIAS

TEA SERVICE LINSIGNIA—Pattern No. 25 "Tea Service" will lend charm to kitchen or breakfast nook—will harmonize with many color schemes.

Notice the smart effect obtained in the kitchen above with the Linsignia, No. 25, "Tea Service."

DURING 1936, a steadily increasing demand for custom effects in linoleum floors made itself felt. Many dealers found that Sealex Linsignias, an ideal answer to this demand, provided them with additional profit on linoleum sales, just as custom-cut border work did.

Unique and attractive, Sealex Linsignias are also extremely moderate in cost and easy to install. You do not even have to restrict yourself to standard designs, one of which is shown here—for practically any design that can be put down on paper can be cut to order in either Sealex Linoleum or Sealex Wall-Covering. Any color scheme can be carried out as these Sealex materials provide such a wide range of beautiful colors.

Remember, the ability to install a custom floor of this type in one special room will help you land orders for other floors in the house.

(above) Congoleum called their precut inlays "Linsignias." Inlay of a tea service is shown in detail and also installed in a floor in a page from a 1937 catalog.

(left) Precut borders offered by Armstrong in 1937 included a ribbon pattern, a Greek key design, a leaf and flower design, and some abstracts. They also cut custom borders at the factory, or their Bureau of Interior Decoration could design one for a customer. They also sold precut border widths for installers to make their own, and it was pointed out that since both patterns were cut at once, a reverse border could be used in another room.

SMART LINOSETS INDIVIDUALIZE FLOORS

Design cut from Nos. 22, 23, 26. Field is No. 27.

No. 025 forms field. Figures cut from No. 23.

Head design in Nos. 23 and 49, on No. 22 field.

Handles, axle are No. 20. Wheel, No. 28. Field, No. 43.

Nos. 21, 28, 41, 42, and 48 in still life effect.

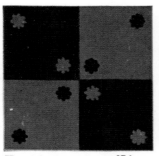

Gay chinaware design executed in Nos. 29 and 48.

How to use reverses of Linosets shown at the right.

Floral design. Flowers cut from No. 40. Field is No. 46.

Lettering cut from No. 23. Field is No. 021.

That Just Corks it

Linoleum is a really wonderful, versatile, amazing, and practical flooring material, but that isn't the only reason to use it, even though that ought to be enough. An even more compelling reason for its use is environmental. It is made from renewable raw ingredients, some of which are already recycled. It lasts a long time if cared for, and once its useful life is over, it can be safely dumped in a landfill for eventual decomposition, it can be composted or incinerated, and though no system has yet been set up, it would be entirely possible to recycle it.

The basic materials from which linoleum is made— linseed oil, desiccants (to help speed the oxidation of the linseed oil), resins, wood flour, powdered cork, ground limestone, pigments, and jute fabric (burlap)—are all renewable, and obtained without major environmental impacts.

(above) Linoleum is both beautiful, like this 1917 Nairn pattern, and environmentally friendly. It is also allergen-free, and because of its antistatic qualities, it actually repels dirt. The continued oxidation of the linseed oil also kills bacteria.

(left) Some Art Deco influence is evident in these 1937 Linosets.

  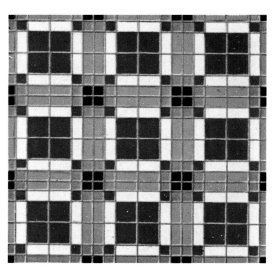

The linseed oil comes from the seeds of the flax plant (that can also be purchased at the local health food store as flaxseed oil), and is grown primarily in Canada and Argentina. In the past, desiccants contained heavy metals such as lead and cobalt, but these have been replaced by relatively harmless manganese compounds (technically a heavy metal, but not exactly Iron Maiden).

The resins (basically tree sap) come primarily from plantation trees that are tapped in the same way that maple trees are tapped for the makings of maple syrup.

Wood flour (fine sawdust) is a by-product of the wood products industry that would otherwise be disposed of in a landfill.

Cork comes from the bark of the cork oak (*Quercus Suber* L), grown primarily in Portugal. The trees live for two hundred years, and must be twenty to twenty-five years old before the bark can be harvested for cork. The sustainable harvesting does not harm the tree in any way; it merely begins growing new bark, which can be harvested again about every ten years. Much of the cork for linoleum production comes from scrap cork produced by makers of bottle corks, or from the shoe industry.

Ground limestone (calcium carbonate or whiting) is available in large quantities throughout the world.

Pigments include titanium dioxide (white), and colored pigments based on iron oxides or organic pigments. (Old linoleum may contain pigments based on heavy metals such as lead, cadmium, or chromium.)

Jute fabric (burlap) is made from the woody fibers of two plants: *Corchorus capsularis* and *Corchorus olitorius,* which are grown mainly in India. In addition, linoleum powder, which is obtained by shredding the scrap linoleum from the production process (the jute fibers are separated and extracted first), is also added to the mix, where it works like sourdough starter to jump-start the oxidation process.

The linseed oil inhibits the growth of microbes, giving linoleum antibacterial qualities. Linoleum also has anti-static properties, so it doesn't attract dirt, unlike plastic, which does.

Contrary to what your mother told you (or what you might remember), linoleum is not difficult to care for: the laborious cleaning and waxing of the past has been rendered obsolete by acrylic sealers that can be applied once a year.

Is there anything bad about linoleum? It costs more than some kinds of vinyl flooring, though about the same as high-end vinyl. It smells of linseed oil initially, though the smell dissipates in a short time. And you can't get it in bright white.

Vinyl Exam

See, I told you there would be a quiz. Actually this is a P.O.P. quiz, which stands for Persistent Organic Pollutants. Vinyl (polyvinyl chloride or PVC) emits toxic compounds during its entire life-cycle, from manufacture to use to disposal. Dioxins are the number one risk from PVC production and disposal. Dioxin is one of the most toxic chemicals ever produced, and causes cancer in smaller doses more than any other chemical. The U.S. Environmental Protection Agency suggests that there is no safe level of dioxin exposure. In addition, PVC manufacturing plants release thousands of pounds of other carcinogenic chemicals into the environment every year, including ethylene dichloride and vinyl chloride. Dioxins also have impacts on the endocrine, reproductive, and immune systems.

PVC requires either plasticizers or stabilizers to be functional. Plasticizers are used to make the vinyl flexible for use in flooring, shower curtains, and the like. The most common stabilizers are called phthalates. Stabilizers are used to slow deterioration of the PVC from heat or sunlight, and include lead, cadmium, and organotins, which are potentially toxic heavy metals (not Def Leppard).

Phthalates are released into the air over time, and can be absorbed through the skin. Asthma has been linked to the phthalates released by vinyl flooring. Phthalates have also been implicated in birth defects.

Lead dust is released from PVC products as they deteriorate in sunlight. Organotins, which cause immune system damage, can leach out of PVC pipes into the drinking water.

Vinyl chloride is also a known carcinogen. One of the largest exposures to vinyl chloride for most people is the new car smell that is produced by offgassing PVC dashboards, door panels, seats, and other parts. Vinyl floors offgas vinyl chloride as well.

As more and more PVC is used in building products, a new hazard has arisen. When PVC burns, it produces hydrogen chloride and dioxin. Hydrogen chloride is lethal when inhaled, and people in burning buildings are often killed by toxic fumes before the flames reach them. This is what the newscasters are talking about when they say someone died of smoke inhalation. Burning vinyl-sided buildings will also release these toxic compounds into the surrounding neighborhood. At the end of its useful life, PVC is the least recyclable of all plastics, the many different additives making recycling impractical and expensive. PVC can contaminate the recycling of other plastics:

Bird Linoleum Company had a few suggestions for brightening up a kitchen on the cheap in this 1950s advertisement, naturally involving the purchase of one of their felt-base rugs (#6325). But look how far we've come-at least women are no longer expected to wear a dress while painting!

This Sloane-Blabon ad appeared in The Progressive Farmer *in 1949, showing the same kitchen three ways. In the first rather fruit-happy example, inlaid pattern #1640 at $3.20 per square yard installed is used. The second features a far less expensive felt-base pattern (#5311), which is only $.89 if you install it yourself. The third uses a green "Marbletone" linoleum at a mere $3.00 per yard installed. The fine print at the bottom mentions "Koroseal" vinyl in "tile, cove base and cove molding."*

one PVC bottle can contaminate a batch of 50,000 PET bottles and render them unrecyclable. There is no safe disposal method for vinyl; if buried in a landfill it will leach toxic chemicals into the groundwater, and if burned, it releases dioxins, heavy metals, and other chlorine compounds that contaminate the air, water, and land.

PVC is unavoidable. Here is a partial list of products that contain PVC: vinyl siding, gutters and drainpipes, water supply pipes, sewage pipes, drainage pipes, electrical conduit pipes; electrical wiring (Romex, insulation on metallic-sheathed cable wires), telephone wiring, data cables, cable sheathing for video, TV, and stereo; vinyl doors and windows; large appliances (PVC shelving, cables, door gaskets); lamp and extension cords, lampshades; computer, fax, and printer casings and cables; vinyl flooring; carpets and mats (vinyl backing); furniture (imitation leather and other parts); miniblinds, shower curtains; food packaging, cling film; tablecloths,

placemats, aprons; shoes and boots; luggage; raincoats, patent vinyl clothing; toys, baby furniture, bibs, diaper covers; garden hoses, garden furniture, tarpaulins, pool toys and inflatable/noninflatable pools; cars (dashboards, door panels, upholstery, etc.); packing tape, ring binders, clipboards, organizers, writing pads; medical items (IV bags, catheters, etc.); LP records (they don't call it vinyl for nothing).

Alternatives have been developed for some of these products, but not all of them. Given the toxicity of the product, it doesn't seem like a good idea to install several hundred square feet of vinyl flooring in your home when there is a better alternative.

Most articles about old linoleum will say that it may contain asbestos. The linoleum rarely contained asbestos, but the adhesives, and sometimes the felt underlayment, could contain asbestos. Armstrong experimented in the 1950s with a synthetic backing fabric called Hydrocord that did contain asbestos. It is best to send a sample of your flooring to a lab and make sure. On the other hand, old vinyl is much more likely to contain asbestos, particularly the old 9 by 9-inch vinyl tiles from the fifties and sixties.

The felt-base products are not without danger. In addition to possible asbestos in the felt, it's highly likely that some of the oil-base paints used to print the designs contained lead, cadmium, chromium, or other heavy metals. Maybe that vintage nursery print felt-base rug wouldn't be quite the right thing for a child's room.

o   o   o

Linoleum couldn't be used in basements because alkaline moisture from the concrete damages the cork filler. The first resilient flooring product made for concrete was asphalt tile. It was composed of asbestos fibers, whiting, inert fillers, and pigments, with an asphalt binder. It was followed by vinyl asbestos tile, basically the same ingredients but with vinyl chloride and plasticizers as the binder. In the 1950s, both of these products were used extensively, especially in basements, as evidenced by this Armstrong illustration of a basement "rec room."

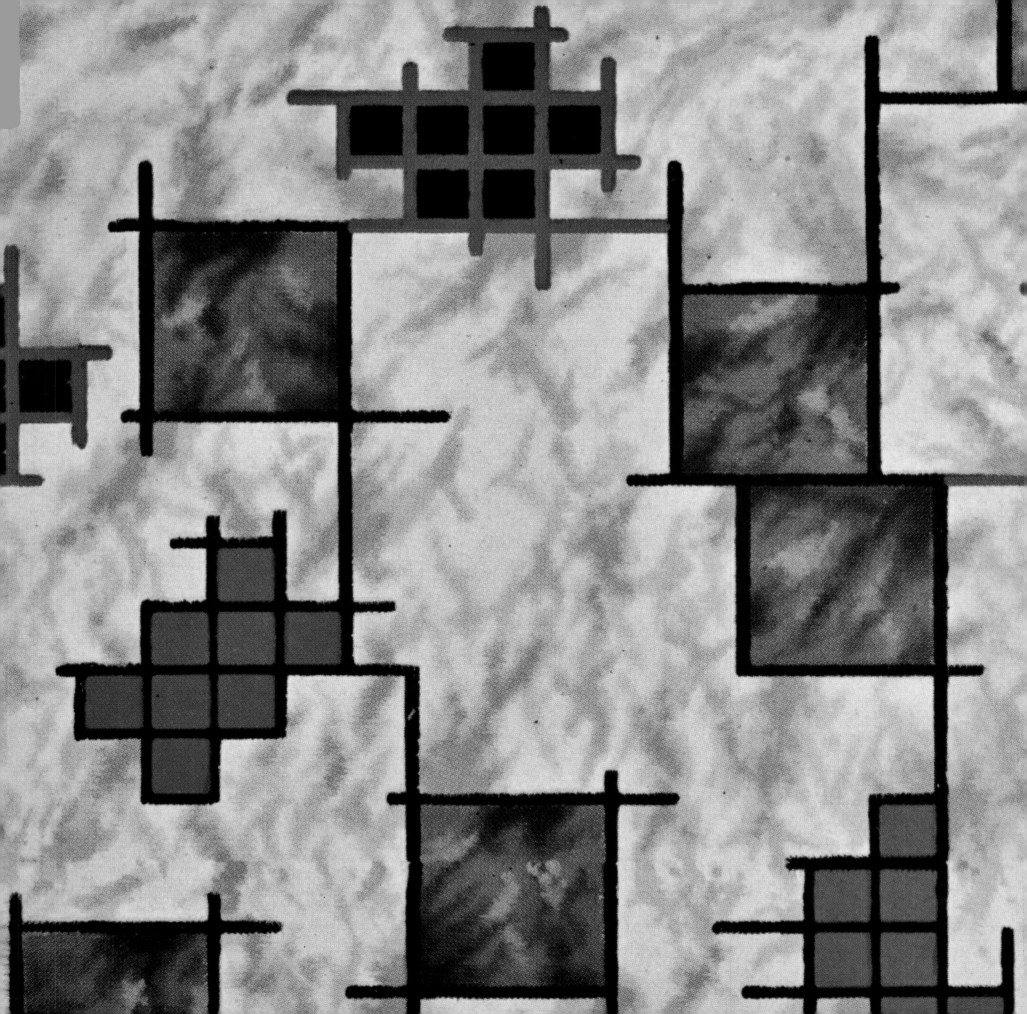

(left) This felt-based Armstrong pattern
(#8769) is from 1937.

(below) An embossed pattern in shades of gray
features acanthus leaves, a decorative motif
usually found on the capitals of Corinthian
columns. (Courtesy of Linoleum City.)

(overleaf) Much of the linoleum produced during the first two decades of the twentieth century had very intricate patterns, such as this
example produced by Nairn in 1917.

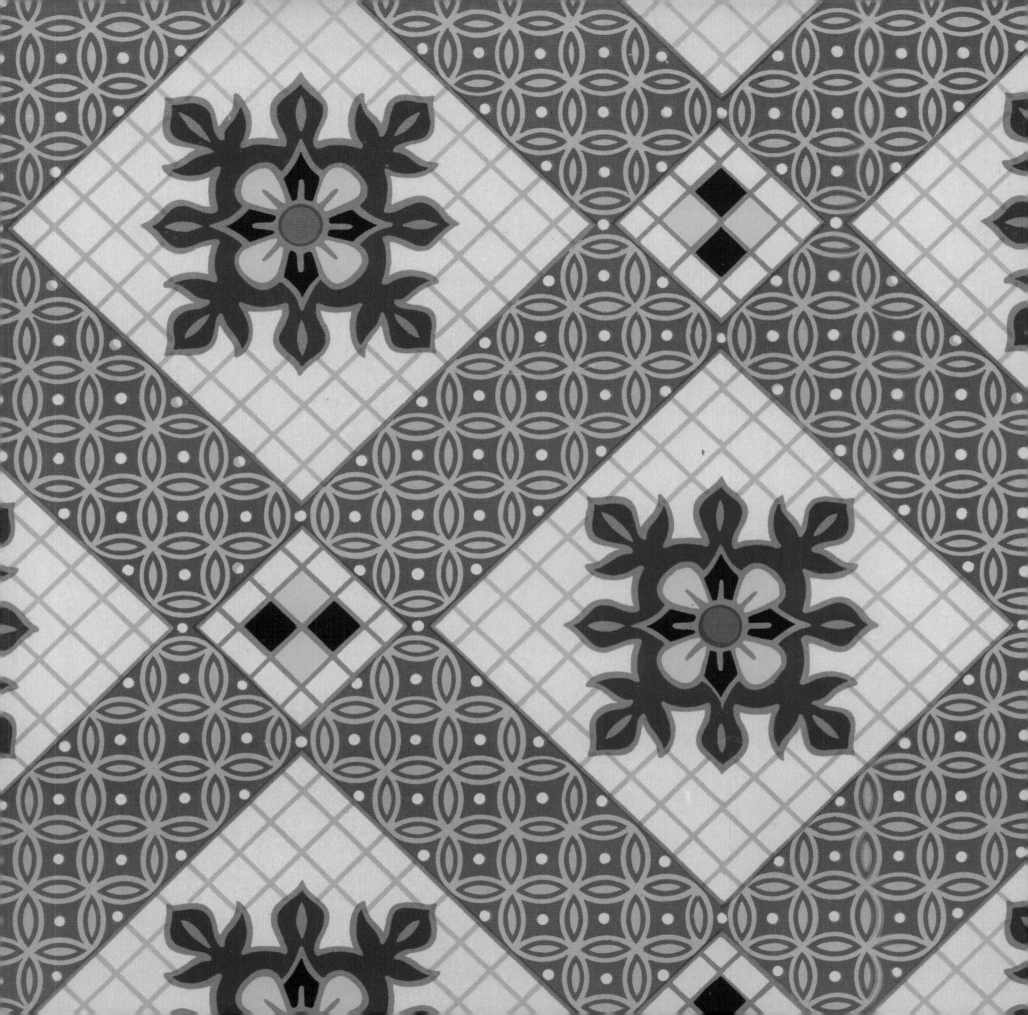

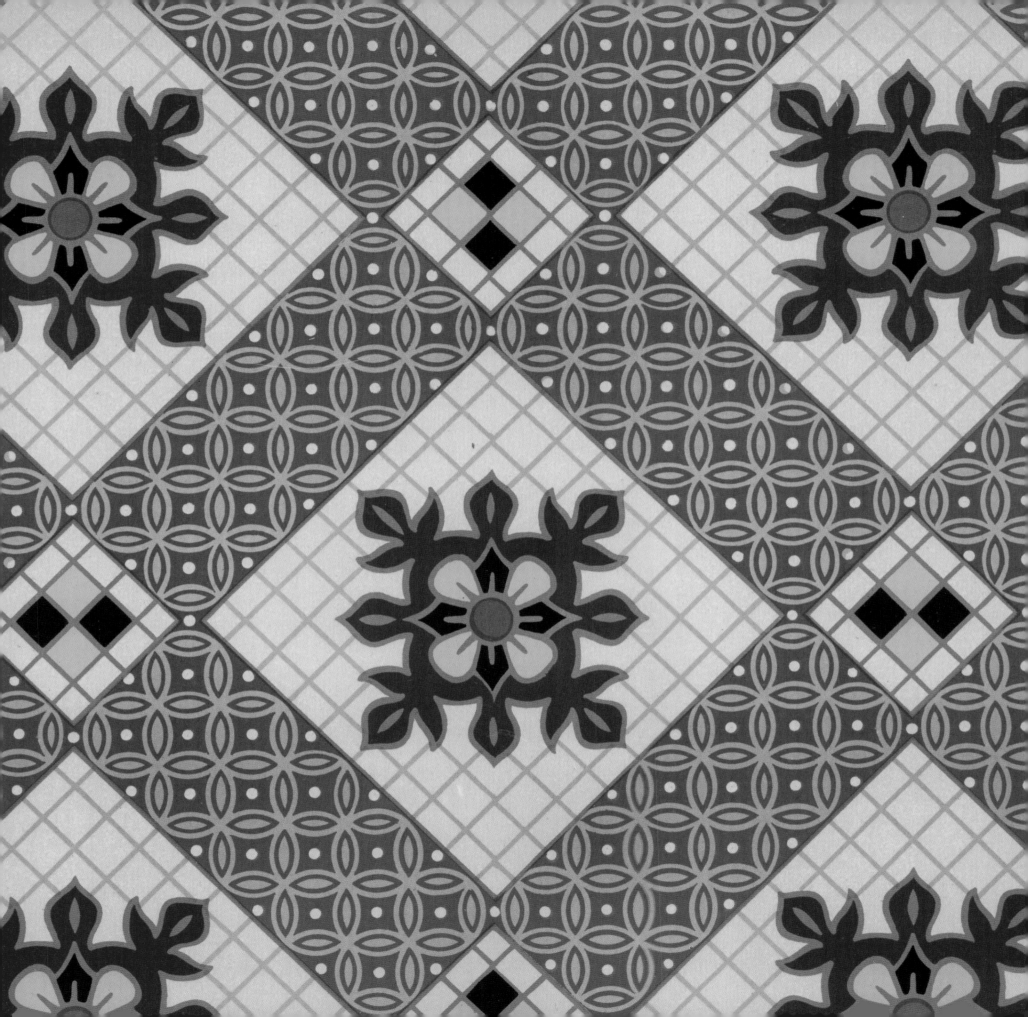

(below) Multicolored leaves on a background of oak leaves in varying shades of gray decorate this piece of printed linoleum. (Courtesy of Linoleum City.)

(right) A tile pattern in inlaid linoleum from the 1917 Nairn catalog has a tailored look.

URINE THE MONEY

Having established that linoleum is a good and wonderful floor covering, there still remains one burning question, at least for those of us with pets: Is linoleum impervious to urine?

A previous cat in my household, having lived long enough (twenty) to become incontinent, clearly proved that vinyl is not impermeable–it went straight through the vinyl and into the particle board subfloor. (Let me just mention here the wonderful powers of shellac for sealing in odors.)

I performed a not very scientific test in which I left a six-inch square sample of linoleum in the cat box for a week. It held up rather well although there was some odor from the back, which I attribute to the burlap wicking up some urine that got underneath. A further test was performed by my friend Friederike and her cat, Biffy, in which a large square of linoleum was repeatedly sprayed and cleaned over a period of six weeks. She concluded that linoleum holds up well with repeated urine spraying and cleaning.

The official word from Forbo and Armstrong is that linoleum is somewhat resistant to urine if it is cleaned up relatively soon. If left there for eight hours it's another story. Cat urine is worse than other kinds because it is more acidic. More coats of sealer will help to protect the floor. If it's too late for that, the best enzyme cleaner to use is Mister Max's Anti-Icky-Poo (www.mister-max.com). (Yes, that is really the name.)

(opposite) Old inlaid linoleum may not stand up as well to urine if the individual pieces have started to separate. Historic linoleum like the 1917 Nairn pattern shown here should be protected from pets if possible, or at least given numerous coats of sealer. Only flexible sealers like acrylic-based products or wax should be used on linoleum—never varnish, shellac, or polyurethane.

RESOURCES

Although this list is as complete as I could make it, I urge everyone to deal locally if possible. Most flooring stores now carry linoleum, though sometimes one must first explain to them the difference between linoleum and vinyl. It may help to ask for the brand name: Armstrong's Marmorette, Domco-Tarkett's Linosom, or Forbo's

Marmoleum. There are many talented installers who do inlay work besides the ones listed here. Often, the flooring store will have a portfolio of work done by their installers, or people that they recommend. Vintage linoleum can occasionally be found in salvage yards or on EBay, but the only guaranteed source is Second Hand Rose.

Purveyors of linoleum:

Armstrong World Industries
2500 Columbia Avenue (17603)
P.O. Box 3001
Lancaster, PA 17604
(717) 397-0611
armstrong.com

Domco Tarkett Commercial
Tarkett Sommer USA
1705 Oliver Street
Houston, TX 77007
(800) 366-2689
(800) 225-6500
tarkettsommerusa.com

Forbo Linoleum, Inc.
P.O. Box 667
Humboldt Industrial Park
Hazleton, PA 18201
(800) 842-7839
themarmoleumstore.com

Linoleum City
5657 Santa Monica Boulevard
Hollywood, CA 90038
(323) 469-0063

Vintage linoleum:

Second Hand Rose
138 Duane Street
New York, NY 10013
(212) 393-9002
secondhandrose.com

Metal linoleum edging for countertops:

Linoleum City
5657 Santa Monica Boulevard
Hollywood, CA 90038
(323) 469-0063

Aubuchon Hardware
95 Aubuchon Drive
Westminster, MA 01473
(800) 282-4393 ext. 2000
aubuchonhardware.com

Do It Best stores
Various locations nationwide
doitbest.com

Penny Lane
1833 N. San Fernando Road
Los Angeles, CA 90065
(323) 222-1200
penny-lane.com

Other flooring manufacturers:

Congoleum Corporation
Department C
P.O. Box 3127
Mercerville, NJ 08619-0127
(800) 274-3266
(609) 584-3000
congoleum.com

Mannington Mills
Corporate Headquaters
Mannington Resilient Floors
Mannington Comercial, Inc.
P.O. Box 12281 (30703)
Calhoun, GA 30721
(800) 241-2262
mannington.com

Linoleum inlay:

Craftsman Design and Renovation
1523 S.E. Taylor Street
Portland, OR 97214
(503) 239-6200
craftsmandesign.com

Inlay Floors
Laurie Crogan
10386 Tupelo Lane
Los Angeles, CA 90077
(310) 474-1821
inlayfloors.com

Custom waterjet and laser cutting for inlay:

Budnick Converting, Inc.
P.O. Box 197
Columbia, IL 62236
(800) 282-0090
budnickconverting.com

Floor Universe, Inc.
210 West Cuyler Street, Ste. 200
Dalton, GA 30720
(800) 599-6897
(706) 275-7060
flooruniverse.com

Precision Laser Cutting
408 Aldo Avenue
Santa Clara, CA 95054
(408) 727-3226
precision-laser.com

Vermont Laserworks
34 Pettingill Road
Essex Junction, VT 05452
(802) 878-1198
vtlaserworks.com

(continued)

Diamonds in green and rust form the perimeter of a linoleum tile floor in a remodeled kitchen. An inlaid striped "rug" adds more color between the sink and the island. (Inlay by Laurie Crogan.)

Convenience wherever you look ..

This kitchen combines a modern layout with the efficiency of a quick-lunch counter. An ingenious arrangement brings range, refrigerator, sink, and work-counter all near at hand, while underfoot is comfortable Armstrong's Linoleum. A crisp, sunny design in Embossed Linoleum No. 5700 provides the key to wall and accent colors—yellow for the walls of washable Linowall, red for chairs and canisters, and gray for counter sides. Such a gay, warm scheme is ideal for a kitchen on the north side of the house, where sunlight may be at a premium.

This illustration from the 1941 booklet Tomorrow's Ideas in Home Decoration *served as the inspiration for the kitchen on page 14. Although the pattern shown (Armstrong #5700) is different, it shares the Art Deco–like squares and "overshot interliners" with the pattern in the actual kitchen.*

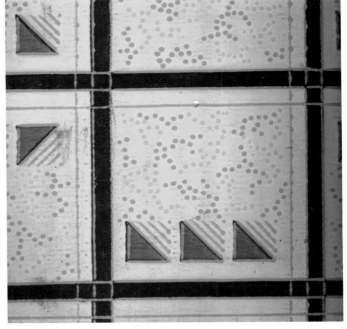

The unabashed favoritism section:

Bungalow Linoleum Floor Idea Page
irvinggill.com/lino.html

Charles Rupert, The Shop
2005 Oak Bay Avenue
Victoria, BC, Canada V8R 1E5
(250) 592-4916
fax (250) 592-4999
charlesrupert.com

Whitehern Historic House and Garden
41 Jackson Street West
Hamilton, ON, Canada L8P 1L3
(905) 546-2018
whitehern.ca/whitehern.php

Information about vinyl toxicity:

Blue Vinyl Toxic Comedy Pictures
200 West 72nd Street #66
New York, NY 10023
(212) 875.0456
bluevinyl.org

Environmental Working Group
1436 U Street N.W., Ste. 100
Washington, D.C. 20009
ewg.org

Greenaction
One Hallidie Plaza, Ste. 760
San Francisco, CA 94102
(415) 248-5010
greenaction.org

Greenpeace
702 H Street N.W., Ste. 300
Washington, D.C. 20001
(800) 326-0959
greenpeaceusa.org

Healthy Building Network
Institute for Local Self-Reliance
2425 18th Street N.W.
Washington, D.C. 20009
(202) 232-4108
healthybuilding.net

Washington Toxics Coalition
4649 Sunnyside Avenue North, Ste. 540
Seattle, WA 98103
(206) 632-1545
watoxics.org

Contact the author:

Jane Powell
P.O. Box 31683
Oakland, CA 94604
(510) 532-6704
bungalowkitchens.com

Contact the photographer:

Linda Svendsen
3915 Bayview Circle
Concord, CA 94520
(925) 676-8299
svendsenphotos.anthill.com

o   o   o

BIBLIOGRAPHY

What do you get when you throw dynamite into an old kitchen?
—Linoleum Blownaparte

Armstrong's Handbook for Linoleum Mechanics. Lancaster, Pennsylvania: Armstrong Cork Company, 1941.

Armstrong's Linoleum, Quaker Rugs, Floor Coverings. Lancaster, Pennsylvania: Armstrong Cork Products Company, 1937.

Brown, Hazel Dell. *Dream Kitchens for 1940*. Lancaster, Pennsylvania: Armstrong Cork Company, 1939.

Brown, Hazel Dell. *Ideas for Old Rooms and New*. Lancaster, Pennsylvania: Armstrong Cork Company, 1944.

Brown, Hazel Dell. *Tomorrow's Ideas in Home Decoration*. Lancaster, Pennsylvania: Armstrong Cork Company, 1941.

Congoleum-Nairn Patterns. Kearny, New Jersey: Congoleum-Nairn, Inc., 1937.

Home Furnishings. Hammond, Indiana: Frank S. Betz Company, 1908.

Forster, Gunter and Josef Eiffler, Uwe Buchholz. *Linoleum*. Munich, Germany: verlag moderne industrie, 1995.

Kaldewei, Gerald, other contributors. *Linoleum, History, Design, Architecture 1882-2000*. Ostfildern-Ruit, Germany: Hatje Cantz Publishers, 2000.

Jester, Thomas C. *Twentieth Century Building Materials*. Washington, D.C.: McGraw-Hill Companies, 1995.

Linoleum Laying Instruction Manual. Kearny, New Jersey: Congoleum-Nairn, Inc.,

Mehler, William A. Jr. *Let The Buyer Have Faith: The Story of Armstrong*. Lancaster, Pennsylvania: Armstrong World Industries, 1987.

Montgomery Ward Catalog # 72. Chicago, Illinois: Montgomery Ward Company, 1903.

Moore, C. Eugene. *Inspiring 1950s Interiors*. Atglen, Pennsylvania: Schiffer Publishing, 1997.

Sloane-Blabon Linoleum and Felt Base. Trenton, New Jersey: Sloane-Blabon Corporation, 1939.

Sloane Quality Linoleum Products. Trenton, New Jersey: Sloane-Blabon Corporation, 1952.

W. & J. Sloane Linoleum and Felt Base. Trenton, New Jersey: W. & J. Sloane Manufacturing Company, 1929.

(opposite) When Swiss art historian Hermann Rothlisberger was quoted as saying, "William Morris would have retracted his dogma of the infallible handicraft if he had been able to see the modern linoleum surfaces," I'm not sure this 1941 Armstrong bathroom is quite what he had in mind.

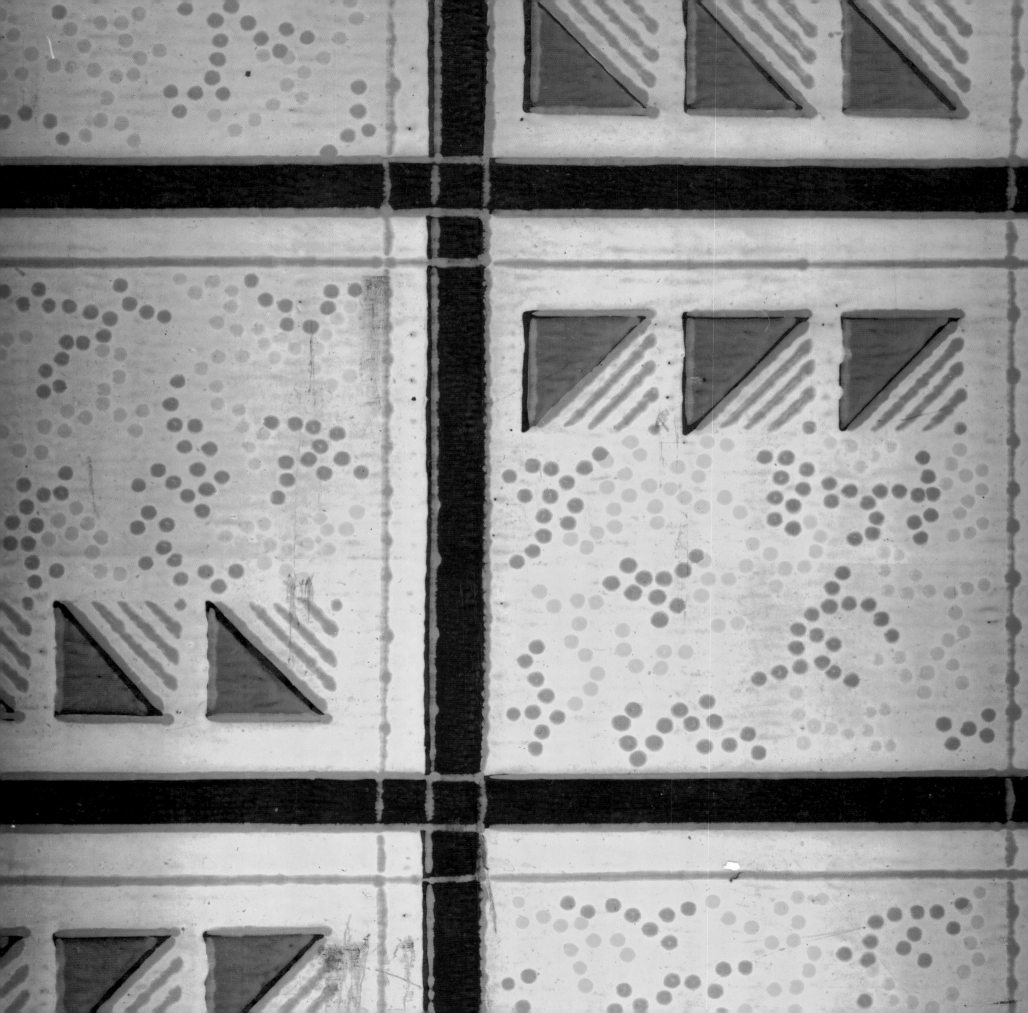

Deep tones of burgundy and green marbleized linoleum contrast with the white cabinets installed in a new vintage-style kitchen built for this old beach bungalow. The stylized border in yellow, green, and black picks up the colors of the tile on the counters and backsplash. The marbling of the linoleum makes even a dark-colored floor easy to keep clean. (Inlay by Laurie Crogan.)

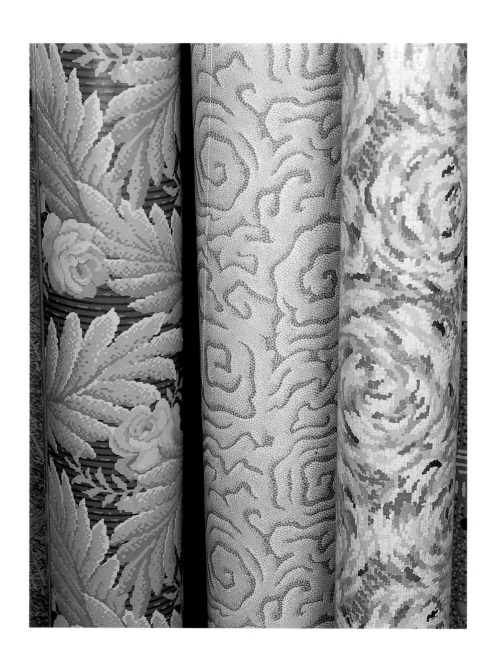

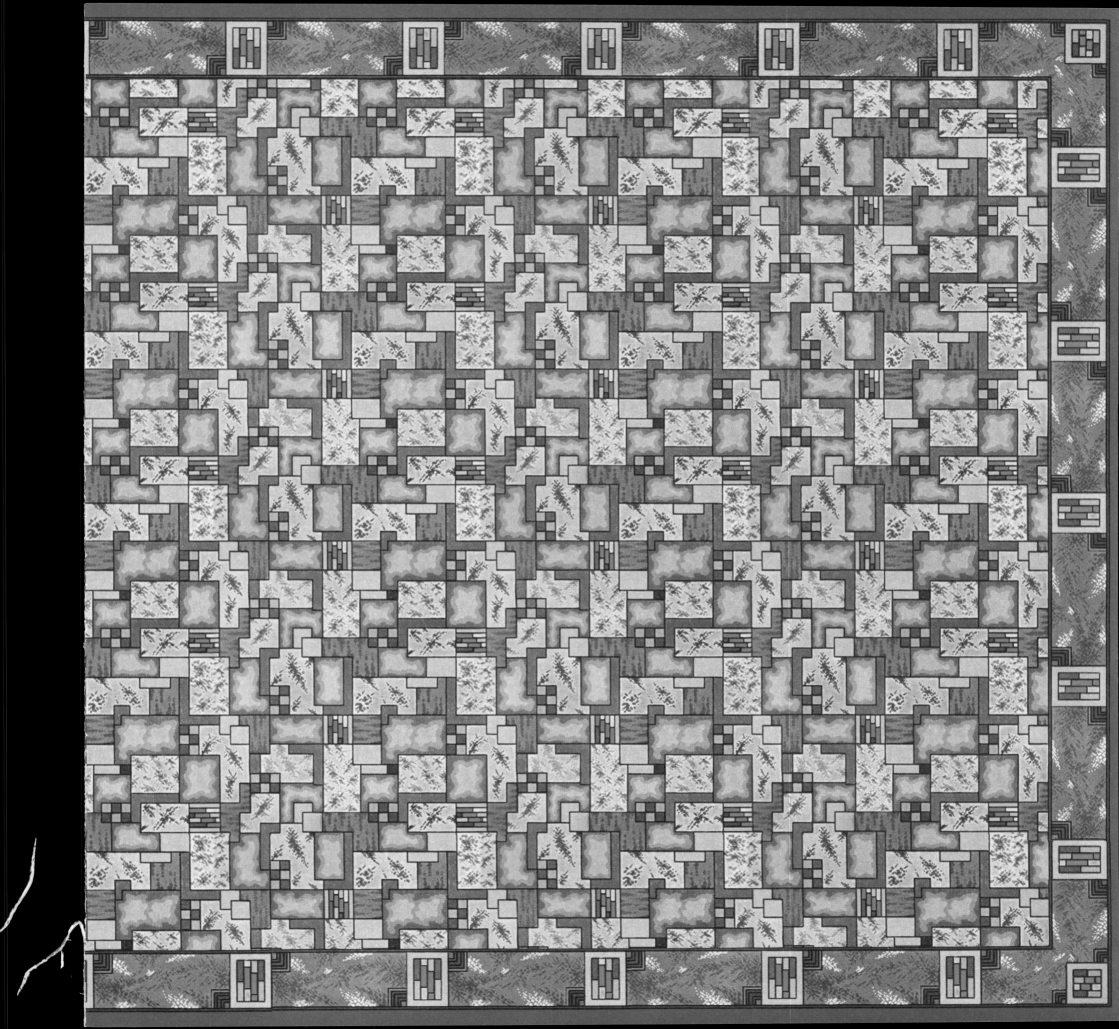

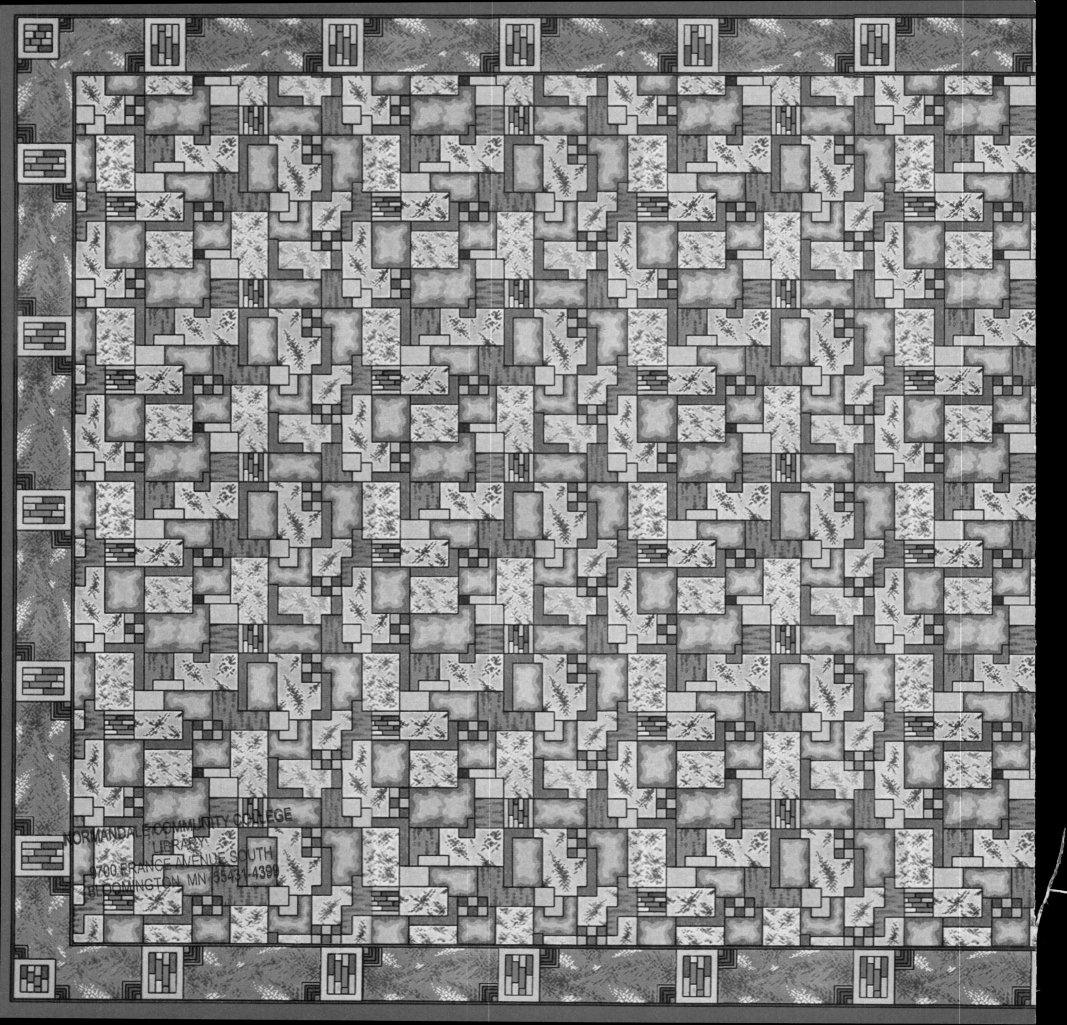